(403) ⌐⌐ ⌐

adrian@adriangeorge.ca

THE DOCTOR'S HANDBOOK

5 Principles of Wealth
You Weren't Taught In Med School

ADRIAN GEORGE

CFP, CLU, TEP

Praise for *The Doctor's Handbook*

"OCCASIONALLY THERE'S A MOMENT WHEN YOU'RE trying to find an answer to a patient's problem and it CLICKS—you've found the solution! Your patient is relieved and so are you. You're thrilled inside that you figured it out! Reading *The Doctor's Handbook* is like that. Adrian has written a solid prescription for financial well-being because he understands the unique challenges doctors face. All you need to do to be rid of sleepless nights worrying about finances is follow his recipe for financial wellness!" —**Dr. Lucas Gursky, Canada.**

"ADRIAN AND PLAYCHEQUES WERE INVALUABLE WHEN we started independent practice. From incorporating (the right way) to taxes, debt repayment, investing, and risk mitigation we were in over our heads immediately. Our education was medical—not financial. Having a responsive team that can be as hands-on or hands-off as we wanted made the transition to practice (and the next steps) easy and much less stressful!" —**Dr. Andrew Dodd, Orthopedic Surgeon, Calgary, AB.**

"As a young professional it was hard to believe some of the stuff Adrian was talking about. In the 15 years since, I'm grateful for his expertise and experience. Adrian helped me navigate some pitfalls and roll with the unexpected. Having him quarterback my financial, insurance, and taxation planning has been great. He understands these worlds and how to navigate them through the different stages of my professional career." —**Dr. Archie Tang, DDS, Calgary, AB.**

"After graduating from optometry school, I realized that I received absolutely zero training with respect to the financial side of being a medical professional. Adrian patiently navigated me through the challenges of financial planning and taught me various strategies to tactfully balance saving for retirement while paying down student debt. I am very grateful for how he has helped to set me up for future financial success!" —**Dr. Clark Tardiff, Optometrist, Calgary, AB.**

———•———

This book is dedicated to my wife Stacia,
who not only encouraged me,
but gracefully (and with more than a few sighs)
put up with many elbow-to-the-ribs moments
as I excitedly shared an idea.

And to our sons,
Damian and Cameron—
I hope this book will inspire you to achieve
your future successes
through helping others.

Note to Readers

I'VE BEEN A FINANCIAL PLANNER FOR OVER 30 YEARS, and working with doctors for the last 20 years. I've seen a lot of what works (and what doesn't!) for doctors. I want this book to help you learn from my experiences, and from the experiences of other doctors. Financial planning is far more than simply investments, and is a combination of both the art and the science of finances. While there is rarely an all-right or all-wrong answer to your many financial questions, there is almost always a head or a heart decision on how you want to approach your debt repayment, lifestyle balance, insurance needs and savings goals. There are the rates and rules now, and what they may be in the future. How you view things now may also be different than in the future. So, applying knowledge of the rules, together with an understanding of what matters to you, and viewing both through the lens of the experiences of your colleagues is your handbook for success.

Your situation is unique, as are your views on risk tolerance. How you view the use of debt or investing in the markets create your financial fingerprint. Consequently, you should never make an investment or other important financial decision without considering your own circumstances and, where appropriate, consulting with your legal or accounting professional advisors. While my goal is to help you make an informed decision yes, or an informed decision no, ultimately it is your decision and you accept sole responsibility for the results of how you use the information I'm sharing with you in this book.

While great care has been taken in the preparation of the information in this book, you agree I cannot be held responsible for errors, omissions, or the results of actions you may take on your own. Nor can I be responsible or accept any liability whatsoever for any loss or damage you may incur, including but not limited to actual loss, or missed opportunity regardless of the legal basis upon which the liability may be based.

I intended this book to entertain, educate and inform. It is not intended to be legal, accounting or specific investment advice for your financial situation.

I hope you enjoy this labour of love, and that it helps you view your options with greater perspectives.

Contents

191 Principle Five: Save It

Foreword

I WAS THRILLED TO FIND OUT Adrian was writing a book to help
doctors with their finances. We learn many things in medical school,
however, learning what's best for our financial future definitely isn't
one of them. I would have signed up for this class!

When my wife Nicki and I started our search for a financial
advisor, we found it a very daunting process. Our primary concerns
were to ensure our children were properly protected, and to avoid
making financial mistakes, so we needed someone we could build
trust with. Someone who not only understood doctors, but also how
busy we are and our need to simplify our lives.

Many advisors had spoken at the university, but they always ended
with a pitch for us to start investing or to buy some insurance. We
wanted someone who would look at our whole picture. To take the
time to understand what was important for us both to achieve, as
well as what to avoid.

We had lots of questions. And once we met Adrian? Those
questions were answered in ways that made sense to us and our
lifestyle.

Since working with Adrian, so much of our financial lives has simplified. He works with our accountant and lawyer to ensure everyone is on the same page before bringing ideas and recommendations back to us. He clears away the noise to allow us to focus on our work and our family.

After years of working together, we regularly meet to ensure our planning is updated to fit our lives, and to keep us on track. Whenever we have a question, we know Adrian can help us no matter what we throw at him.

Our relationship has grown into a true partnership in our financial success and we no longer worry about what the future holds for our family.

This book is like your new financial-life-plan Merck Manual!

Dr. Ryan Martin, M.D.
Orthopedic Trauma and Arthroscopic Knee Surgeon
University of Calgary, AB. Canada

Principle One: Plan It

What is measured, is managed.

CHAPTER 1

Three Surprising Reasons Why I Only Work With Doctors

LET'S SEE. YOU'RE A DOCTOR WHO spent many years in university and med school. You have a student loan that would make most people have a panic attack. You're either new to practice or you've been at it for a while, and now you really want to make all that time, effort, and investment work for you.

I get it.

I also know you were taught all sorts of amazing and difficult things in med school.

But creating and managing wealth certainly weren't on the curriculum.

I hear this often from my clients,

"Adrian, they never taught me any of this stuff in med school!"

Don't worry about it. We all have our crazy paths to where we are now.

Before I started my own business, I worked at four major banks in Canada, initially as a part-time teller, then as manager, as one of a divisional management team, and finally as a regionally assigned financial planner who assisted branches with their more complicated planning needs. And while the banks are all different in many ways, they also have many similarities.

And it's why I stepped away from them.

The frustrations and lessons I've experienced—they're why I set out to be independent so I could put you, and all of my doctor clients, at the centre of everything I do.

Before I dive into the nuts and bolts of the rules of managing your wealth—I'll give you a quick backstory of what led me to writing this book. For YOU.

Because now? *I only work with doctors—and you'll soon see why.*

First Up? I Didn't Like How Banks Saw Doctors:

1. You're only a number and sales target.

At the last major bank I worked, financial planners at the branch had to have at least 450 clients on their desks. If they didn't have that many, clients were picked from a Senior Account Manager and plunked onto the financial planner's desk. It made me wonder how they could possibly meet with that many people in a year and spend the appropriate amount of time assessing their needs?

Answer: They couldn't. It isn't possible.

Those same bank financial planners also had to have seven products per client. I hated how this was referred to as having a 'larger share of the wallet' … your wallet, that is. I really disliked weekly sales meetings, where my manager reviewed who I met with that week and discussed any 'missed sales opportunities'.

Doctors were always on that list.

You go into your bank to get advice on how to allocate your income most effectively and you receive the planning equivalent of the 'would you like fries with that' upsell.

That's a hard pass from me, thanks.

2. Bank incentive programs may not align with what's best for you.

I know many wonderful people at the banks from all my years working there. They care about their clients, and want to see them succeed. But I also know compensation ultimately drives behaviour. The planners at the bank I worked at had a base salary, and received a bonus on the value of both their assets under management as well as debts like mortgages and loans.

This created at best, a financial disincentive, at worst, a conflict of interest.

Should you take money out of your investments to pay down or pay off your debts? Maybe, maybe not. But the planners I worked with would have taken a double-hit to their bonus if you did.

I'm not saying for one moment that most of them wouldn't give you the right advice.

But I found it distasteful that their compensation model encourages one answer over another.

This is why my clients can choose to simply pay an hourly or yearly flat fee for their planning—it removes all conflicts of interest.

I'll never forget the first time I was a bank manager back in the 90s, and a new Asian Pacific mutual fund was being launched. During its launch, I was told in order to attract the portfolio manager the bank wanted to manage this new fund—they'd assured the portfolio manager they'd have at least $50 million in it within a couple of years.

WHOA.

Guess what became part of every client's recommended portfolio?

The only difference I saw in portfolio recommendations was the percentage amount to be invested within this new mutual fund. If you had a time horizon longer than five years and could handle some fluctuation in your portfolio, this product was being recommended to you.

It was an eye opener for me. I'm grateful it happened early in my career so I could apply the right lens to viewing investment recommendations with a critical eye to what makes the most sense for YOU, not the investment company.

The Know-Your-Client B.S. Questionnaire Doesn't Fit Doctors

If you've done any investment with a legitimate investment company, you've undoubtedly been walked through their *Know Your Client* (KYC) questions.

These questions are typically:

» How long do you have before you need your money?

» What have you invested in before?

» What's your level of investment knowledge?

» How much of a loss could you tolerate?

I remember having a battle royale with my compliance officer on how minimal and ineffective KYCs are. Don't get me wrong, I strongly believe in compliance. In fact, I used to be a back up divisional compliance officer for a major bank brokerage. But I couldn't set aside what both my training and experience was overwhelmingly showing me—KYCs were almost useless and not good for much more than ticking a box to say you had agreed to their recommended investment portfolio.

Here are three reasons why:

1. Only two questions ever changed the end results significantly. Unless you'd never invested before, or couldn't tolerate any loss, the majority of outcomes resulted in a client being considered balanced-growth (typically 60% stocks, 40% fixed income).

Your entire portfolio was invested with the same cookie cutter approach they gave everyone else.

The banks often don't assess that as a doctor, you're likely to treat your investments for retirement differently than for your children's education, despite both being usually more than five years away. Your savings in your company are also taxed differently than savings you may hold personally, and be considered "passive income" with a 50% bite held on deposit with the government. Where you hold your assets and in what accounts is critical for doctors, but the banks I worked at never reviewed how a doctor's practice has special financial needs.

2. If I asked you what amount of risk (loss) you could handle when the markets shoot up, or after they've dropped significantly, would you have the same answer? I know I wouldn't.

Being asked how much risk you can tolerate will vary greatly, depending on if you feel euphoric when your portfolio is up, or anxious because you've suffered a loss already. And because you spent so many years in med school, your timelines are different than normal investors anyway.

3. There were never any cash flow questions I encountered, or other types of investment preferences.

How secure do you, and maybe your partner, feel in your income streams? How might your investment strategy change if either of your work was interrupted for a few months? How much more important to you is funding your children's RESPs over your retirement goals?

Sorry, these and so many other relevant questions aren't on any KYC I've ever seen.

These Two Doctors Were Frustrated

The final banking straw for me came when I was referred to work with Rebecca and her husband Tom. Rebecca was a newly practicing doctor who had just moved to Calgary, and they wanted to buy a home. They met with a Senior Account Manager (SAM) to help them get a mortgage, and the SAM noticed they had savings at another bank and wanted my help to bring those assets over.

When I met with Rebecca and Tom, I could see they were quite frustrated. I immediately threw out my meeting agenda and asked them what was on their minds.

"I don't know why I'm here!" said Rebecca. "I just wanted to get a mortgage, but everyone keeps talking about our savings."

Can you relate?

It was early 2009. The markets had taken a beating in the previous year—the Toronto Stock Exchange dropped 35% in what became known as The Great Recession.

Rebecca and Tom had been told to invest toward their down payment, but they lost money. They saved more of their earnings to recover, and were now being asked to invest it *again* when all they wanted was to finally buy their home.

Not only did they have anxiety from the markets—they also wanted to save money for a planned maternity leave.

No wonder they were so upset ... so was I!

During our planning I also noticed Rebecca hadn't become incorporated yet, as they'd just moved and started her practice. I went to our branch to inquire about the tax rates for incorporated doctors, and how we could use her Professional Corporation to help their planning. She proceeded to show me yet another investment plan she wanted me to show Rebecca and Tom.

I wouldn't do it.

Rebecca and Tom had many moving parts in their lives; from a new practice to buying a first home, becoming incorporated and starting a family. None of their immediate concerns were about investing for their retirement, but that's what everyone kept talking to them about.

I wanted to give them the experience they deserved, and to put their needs at the centre of everything I recommended for them. I respected their money and knew they'd worked hard for it.

After I helped Rebecca and Tom get on track with their mortgage (and ignored everything my manager gave me), we went to work on how to best plan for their desire to start a family. I have a whole chapter on what we needed to consider coming up later.

After this experience, I was at home and really thinking about who I enjoyed working with.

It certainly wasn't the bank.

I assessed every account (I mean every.single.one.) and which clients were the best to work with.

And at the top of the list?

Doctors were the clients I enjoyed helping the most.

Doctors have lives and businesses filled with many moving parts, so they need someone to make their financial lives easier, without the constant upsells.

So, after much reflection, I left the world of banking to help them.

And I've never looked back.

———◆———

Why do I focus exclusively on the unique challenges and opportunities of medical professionals?

Most people would say,

"It's because doctors make a lot of money!"

Well. So do many professionals. That wasn't the reason.

3 Reasons Why I Love Working With Doctors:

1. **You love the work you do.** Sure, it has its challenges and frustrations, but I've never met a doctor who didn't love their work. I enjoy being around people who are as passionate about helping others as I am.

2. **You're used to working on a team.** Doctors are trained as a team to work collaboratively. You utilize the skillsets of others to add to problem-solving for your patients. I like to operate the same way by working with your financial team of an accountant, lawyer, or lender.

3. **I look through the lens of what I've seen work for your colleagues.** While each of you are different and with individual needs, goals, and concerns—there are also many similarities. You get the benefit of my experience with other doctors, of what has worked, or what to avoid. It helps me build the trust that's so important for your financial security.

Your financial world has become incredibly complex.

In the last ten years alone, you've seen huge tax rate increases, active or passive business income definitions, and even a tax on NERDs. (Well, not quite. That's the *Non-Eligible Refundable Dividend Tax on Hand*, but it still takes the government to come up with a name like that.)

The biggest change in working with doctors came in 2017.

The Federal Government had just announced their intent to bring out the *Tax on Split Income* rules (TOSI), designed to prevent you from reducing your household income tax by not allowing you to pay a dividend to a lower-taxed spouse or partner. This wasn't good news! Before 2017, this was a key benefit for becoming incorporated; I've seen literature from the government on how to set yourself up to do this income-splitting with your partner.

In 2017, the government language told me you were now in their cross-hairs.

In 2013, if you needed $200,000 of household income, you could expect to pay around $40,000 of household income tax by allocating some of your income to your partner through a dividend. Now? Today's tax rates and TOSI prevent you from paying a dividend to your partner, and your tax bill has shot up to over $55,000 (a 37% increase!).

"I rob banks because that's where the money is."
—Willie Sutton

Willie is the government, and you're their bank.

I felt the rug had been pulled out from under my doctors' feet.

Understandably, my doctor clients fired all sorts of questions at me.

» What did this mean for their ability to save for a down payment?

» How about funding their children's education?

» How would this affect their retirement, and should they still be incorporated?

My doctors needed me to be more than just a means to safeguard and grow their savings. They needed me to become their Chief Financial Officer who advised them on all areas of their financial health and wealth like: how and when to incorporate, what's deductible, what insurance they needed, what debt they should get rid of to free-up cash-flow, and how best to save for their children's education, retirement, or estate planning.

And as my clients' children grow, they often look to me for advice on how to help their children appreciate financial opportunities and make wise decisions so they can stand on their own two feet.

Bye-Bye Weird Little KYC Form. Hello My What-Really-Matters-to-You Form

If you're wondering what tool I use to help you get started, let's just say I needed a few pots of coffee to create it.

You see, your time is valuable and I never want to waste it.

Our time together shouldn't be spent on things I can read on a statement, or have you wait as I sift through your mortgage documents.

Instead, I focus on your gut.

Your Most Important Financial Strategy Comes From Your Gut

What IS important in our time together, is how you FEEL about certain things.

Just because you have a mortgage and a RESP tells me nothing about how you feel about your priorities in allocating your money between them.

On one side of your financial decisions are what the numbers dictate is your best option, and on the other side is what your gut tells you. Sometimes these are in alignment, other times not. For many of my doctors, the answer is somewhere in-between.

The secret to proper financial planning is the ability to make an informed yes, or an informed no, that finds YOUR balance between head and heart. You're going to read more about this in Chapter 2!

Three Head and Heart Questions:

1. **What's important about money to you?** Often, I hear things like: security; or being able to make a purchase without worrying about its long-term impact. The freedom to do what you want when you want, while also knowing your goals are being achieved and concerns avoided.

2. **What are tangible goals for you and your family that require both money and planning to achieve?** Ah, now we're getting somewhere. Whether it's a home renovation or planning a memorable family trip, we're getting to what matters to you.

3. **When you contemplate the use of debt for a major purchase, what factors do you take into consideration?** This allows me to understand your mindset better. Is it interest rates? Is it cash flow? Is it a purchase you've always wanted, even if it's not always financially driven? We dive into your money habits and what drives them.

My questions for you aren't on a statement or a yes or no tick-box that just fills out a compliance form. I want to know how you want your life to unfold. And then I help you get there.

This book asks questions that allow you to focus on what you want, and avoid the "Would you like fries with that?" upsell.

As one of my clients Richard says,

"My greatest concern now is deciding what wine to have with dinner."

I love it! Let's get started!

———•———

"At last! Something that goes well with us!"

Chapter Summary Lessons:

1. Work with someone who works with doctors, and views you as a person not a dollar sign.

2. Understand their motivation—why do they want to work with you?

3. Your best financial plan balances both your head and your heart.

CHAPTER 2

Let Your Head or Heart Decide It

EVERY SINGLE LIFE DECISION YOU MAKE comes from a Head vs Heart position.

What's right for you, forms your unique money habits. Once you know your habits, your choices become easier to make.

If you always choose to follow your HEAD:

You want a logical, predictable, and safe outcome. (But you may secretly wish that you could have more freedom.)

If you always choose to follow your HEART:

You believe in living your passions, but you also may secretly worry about ending up living in a van down by the river.

Think about some of the decisions you've made in your life.

Have you ever procrastinated on a decision, unsure of which choice was best? Was it easier to simply shove it in a corner and focus on other things? (Please tell me I'm not the only one!)

Or you made a decision not because it was the best choice, but rather one you felt wasn't a "wrong" choice and it felt safer?

What most people do in this situation is DO NOTHING, rather than risk making a "wrong" decision. But they've traded one problem for another: losing the time needed to achieve their goals.

Doing nothing is a decision. People will keep doing what they've always done if they don't clearly see a major benefit of change/choice done today.

But even more importantly than knowing it? **You have to feel it.**

Financial planning can become confusing and so it often gets shoved under the rug.

But delaying a decision can cost you, whether it's seeing your desired home go up in price, missing an investment opportunity that turned out great, or even simply continuing to pay a high interest rate while you've got cash sitting in your bank account.

Don't beat yourself up. We've all done it.

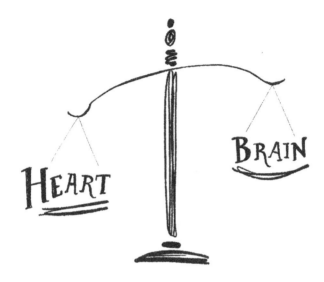

You're on the weigh scales of Head vs Heart. The good news is you can have both.

———•———

Contrary to what you may have been told, in your financial planning there's rarely an all-right or all-wrong answer to the many questions you're going to have.

I know this is frustrating when there's not always a clear winner to pick. But in my experience, it's also liberating for you! Knowing there's rarely an all-wrong answer helps you to take action, rather than be paralyzed about making the 'wrong' choice.

Remember. It's not that there's a right or wrong answer, it's that you usually have a *numerical winner or a preference winner.*

Both have their individual pros and cons and the trick in creating your plan is to find out where between your two points best fits with you.

And there's always a way to make it happen.

Meet Jason. A Stressed-Out Surgeon.

Recently I was out for coffee with one of my surgeons who, like so many of my newer clients, has both a student line of credit and another LOC for some unexpected home renovations.

With interest rates on the rise, he saw more and more of the household income going to service the interest on these lines of credit, to the tune of over $3,000 per month in interest. Yikes.

Jason set down his coffee and shook his head.

"Adrian, is there a numerical tipping point when it makes more sense to pay down our lines of credit rather than keeping our income in my Prof Corp? I really don't like paying a lot of tax, but I can't stand seeing so much money disappearing in interest."

I said, "The math on this is pretty clear, but it won't be what makes your decision for you. When the tax rate you pay is the same as your interest rate, that's the tipping point numbers-wise.

The real answer is how it's already impacting you when you should experience the rewards of finally being able to practice."

Should Jason Go With His Head Or Heart?

I could have told Jason how it's better to only pay his small business rate of 11%, rather than 42% or more personal tax rate, and have the 30+% difference growing and compounding in his company. Over time he'd be able to ride out the ups and down of the markets, and he'd be much further ahead.

BUT.

He'd probably have huge bags under his eyes from losing sleep worrying about his debt.

Jason's head was telling him it was better to grow his net worth faster by not paying a third of his income in excess tax. But his heart wasn't having any of that.

"Listen Jason, I don't want you spending ten years waking up at 2 a.m. because your debt upsets you.

If it means working two more years to get the savings goal you want, but you're more relaxed along the way because we hammered your debt, how would that feel?"

"I don't like paying so much tax, but I just can't stomach not getting rid of my debt faster. If you're saying the real choice is be stressed but retire faster, or have less stress and work a couple more years—I think I could do those years easily," Jason replied.

"Then let's not let the tax-tail wag the dog, Jason," I said.

We set a plan in motion that day to tackle his lowest line of credit, then the next, and finally his largest. As a nod to his desire to also save and reduce his income taxes, we opted for three quarters of his extra income towards debt (as it would be less after personal tax), and the remaining amount towards his corporate savings that he would only pay 11% tax on.

This was the blend Jason needed to find his balance between his head versus heart battle.

———•———

You're certainly not alone in feeling confused about what to do with your money.

For many of the doctors I've worked with over the years, it's been less about *making the 'best' choice* and more about *not making the 'wrong' one* (and discovering it years later!).

The fear of making a wrong decision can prevent us from starting ANYTHING. It can paralyze us. Which feels even stranger when you're used to making big decisions on a daily basis. (As a doctor, you deal with people's health issues, which is as big as it gets.)

If you're having difficulty in making your planning a "today" issue for you, it's time to consider this mind bender.

The Power of 240

I want to give your thinking a twist.

Think *less* that you have twenty long years of work ahead of you and *more* that **you only have 240 months** to make the most of all your hard work.

Weirdly, 240 months isn't that long.

You can actually *feel* the months ticking away. And the longer you procrastinate to get going?

Those remaining months have to do even heavier lifting. Losing time as you delay making choices can significantly impact how quickly and comfortably you become financially independent, often as much as making a wrong decision does.

This doesn't mean you shouldn't have a moment's pause before taking action, but instead use the power of 240 to motivate you to get your financial plan created. It guides you to make better decisions faster, and maximize the months you have.

What Would You Do With An Extra $10K A Month?

What would your head and heart tell you to do, if you had an extra $10,000 per month, and you could put it toward additional mortgage payments or increase your savings in your company?

You've probably heard the earlier you can get your money growing and compounding, the better. You've also likely heard that becoming debt free quickly is a cornerstone of financial health.

Which option is right?

Would it surprise you to learn they BOTH can be right? (And what IS being right anyway?) A better question is **"Which option is right for me?"** Sometimes paying debt can be the best answer for you, while sometimes building your savings is the best option.

Your financial plan must let you sleep well at night, while still making progress toward your goals.

It's the balance I encourage my clients to strive for.

So how can you determine what's your 'best choice'?

Keep reading!

I'll share the secrets I've learned after many years of working with doctors. I'll help you better understand your options ahead, so you can make an informed decision that best balances your goals and values.

There's rarely an all-right or all-wrong choice in your financial plan, if it reflects your unique head versus heart balance.

Creating your financial plan using your head and heart is much easier than you think. Just like how Jason wrestled with what to do with his head versus heart struggle around his student debt or savings decision, we can find your unique blend.

And if your views or situation changes, so too can your blend. The secret is to get started on a plan that makes sense for you.

As for Jason? He's no longer the stressed-out surgeon.

He sees his savings going up while his debts are going down!

—•—

Chapter Summary Lessons:

1. There isn't a right or wrong answer. Understand your head and heart options, and where you fit in-between them.

2. View your working career as shorter lengths of time to build your motivation.

3. You can always change if your views change.

CHAPTER 3

60% It.

WHAT DOES THE NEXT FIVE YEARS look like for you? The next ten? The next twenty?

When I ask this question of my clients, it's usually easy for them to tell me what they see happening over the shorter term. They start squirming when we look at a longer time frame. Twenty years seems like a very long time away! (Remember when you were twenty and thought forty was old?)

But here's a question for you, now that you think of only having 240 months left:

Do you want to spend them all working as hard as you do now?

I admit when I first thought of my career this way, I felt both a sense of urgency to work hard and make the most of my potential, as well as a desire to maximize my time with my young family. It felt unachievable. Like something would always be sacrificed.

You've heard the phrase before: Life Balance.

The problem is, I don't believe this is the best way to view the question of how you want to use your 240 months. Let me explain.

How do your goals and values stack up?

You almost certainly receive a lot of meaning and value in your work helping others. You also value time away with your family and friends. So, the question isn't really about the time you allocate between work and life, but rather how your goals and values for each of these areas *stack against each other*.

The more you put to debt, the more your debt stack shrinks. But then you're working non-stop, and you don't take many holidays or see your family much.

The more you prioritize time off, your goals for debt freedom and financial independence are delayed.

This can cause quite an internal conflict!

Maybe you're fresh out of school and you want to run hard and fast to eliminate your debt and save as much as you can, as quickly as possible.

Or maybe you feel like you want to have more dedicated time off now, because you love to travel. But you're unsure how that will impact your financial goals.

Let's flip this craziness with a simpler question:

What if you were to define what you NEED to earn vs what you CAN earn?

Because they absolutely aren't the same thing.

Imagine Only Needing To Work 60% Of Your Current Workload

I met with Chris, a doctor mid-stream in his career, and he looked exhausted.

"No matter what I do, there's never enough time. Even meeting with you today I had to reschedule several times. Something urgent always comes up," Chris said. "I've paid off my debt and need to save as quickly as possible."

I smiled at him, as this poor guy looked like he could fall out of his chair.

"Chris, you've done an excellent job in getting rid of your debt. I know it can feel like you're in the home stretch to save as much as possible so you can stop before you feel completely burnt out. Every day you field questions from residents, respond back to patients, deal with staff and have a schedule that's constantly being reshuffled on you. You also have a young family and want to avoid being MIA with them. You're carrying a lot on your shoulders."

"You're struggling with competing priorities, and you feel you're in a race against burnout to save as much as you can to be able to retire as quickly as possible. Am I right?"

Chris looked at me with a tired grin and said, "You nailed it!"

You see, every advisor Chris had met had assumed he only cared about how big he could grow his pot. Nobody had asked him how big a pot he needed in the first place.

So, he felt it was a race against time to save as much as he could toward an unknown goal, and before burning out.

To paraphrase Robert Lowell, sometimes the light at the end of the tunnel is an oncoming train.

"There's light at the end of the tunnel but it looks like the bulb's gone."

We needed to switch tracks, and fast.

Otherwise, Chris would need to leap like James Bond before the train crashed. We didn't want that kind of drama.

He needed a train with a scenic route toward a planned destination. Chris could take a little longer to get where he wanted to go and enjoy the journey along the way.

This financial journey was what THIS doctor was ordering.

"Chris, when I look at your planning, I don't think you need to work as hard as you are. Actually, we could have you retire within ten years working just a little over half of your workload now."

Chris was quiet for a minute—from shock.

He looked at me and said,

"You're the first person to ever tell me I don't have to work as hard as I am."

Chris Moved Into The 60% Lane

What followed next was a complete 180-degree change in how he viewed work.

Once Chris knew how much he *needed* to earn each month for his planning, he felt liberated.

If he chose to work more than he needed to that month, he felt like he was *accelerating* his plan not working *for* his plan. Even his vacations were now guilt-free. He'd earn what he needed to earn that month, and then if he spent a couple of weeks away with his family, his plan was unaffected.

Chris felt so much more in control, and he had the freedom to say "no."

———•———

Your work life balance isn't a trade off with one side winning at the expense of the other.

Your work life balance is created by the amount you *can* earn vs the amount you *need* to earn.

I love seeing how this kind of mind shift lifts a burden from my clients and gets them reinvigorated for their work. They see it as getting ahead of their planning, rather than just working FOR their planning.

This simple mind-shift puts you in the driver's seat. You get to decide what feels right, without fear of making a 'wrong' decision. *And you can change it at any time.*

Feels great, doesn't it? Once you feel in control of those 240 months, it feels pretty amazing. Now, when I meet with Chris, he's laughing and smiling as he tells me about the adventures he's enjoying with his family.

I really look forward to our meetings!

What's the right work and life balance for you?

You may thrive on getting to financial independence as quickly as possible, or you may want to take your foot off the gas pedal a little bit and take in the scenery.

There is no right or wrong answer here.

Start with knowing what you need to earn for your plan. And what you can earn above that number? Save more, spend more, live more, or pay down more … any or all of these, it's totally your call!

And doesn't the sound of working at only 60% speed feel better?

———•———

Chapter Summary Lessons:

1. It's the difference between what you CAN earn vs what you NEED to earn, that powers your work & life balance.

2. When you know what you need to earn, you'll feel encouraged to accelerate it but not feel guilty if you take more time for yourself.

3. You're more likely to stay on track and achieve your goals if you're not wearing a straitjacket.

Principle Two: Keep It

You've worked hard to earn your income.
Now keep it.

Incorporate It

WHAT WOULD YOU GUESS IS THE #1 reason WHY you should incorporate?

To defer paying tax.

"As your accountant I'd advise you to
hunt, gather, and invent the tax shelter."

If you earn over $50,000 per year in *excess* of what you need for your personal debt and lifestyle spending, I likely will want you to become incorporated.

By keeping income sheltered from your higher personal tax rate under the umbrella of your company *rather* than paid to you directly—the money you'd otherwise give to the government works for you instead. (Money you'd never see again, otherwise.)

Ideally, you'll save your excess income in your company while your tax rates are higher, and you're able to withdraw it later when your income needs are lower. When your debt is gone or your kids are out on their own.

Most likely though, in my experience, you'll always be at or near the higher tax rates, even when retired!

I started working with a newly practicing surgeon, who shared how many of his colleagues were wondering if it even made sense to incorporate anymore. I get it—governments have painted a big red target on the backs of doctors.

Incorporating can give you some big benefits though. It is still worth doing.

How does Incorporating Help You?

What would you do with 70% more of your income?

I knew that would catch your attention.

When you're incorporated, you can pay yourself the income you need for your lifestyle and debt repayment goals.

Any of your income you don't pay out as a salary or expense and choose to keep within your company is called "retained earnings." In Alberta, your retained earnings are currently taxed at 11% on your first $500,000, and 23% for income above $500,000 you retained that year. Compare that to paying up to 48% tax if you received your income personally.

Put another way, you could have up to 70% more of your income working to grow your net worth!

Do you need help off the floor?

Meet Jonathan and Marcus. Which One Is Right?

Jonathan and Marcus are friends who are both starting out on their careers. Jonathan plans on getting incorporated.

Marcus doesn't see the point. With so many rules in place, extra accounting, and legal needs, and generally a sense of confusion around why becoming incorporated benefits him, he'd rather keep things simple. If he could be on a salary tomorrow, he'd take it.

This makes Jonathan start to question if what he always assumed he should do—get incorporated—is worth doing, after all.

Jonathan is the one who is right.

Marcus is missing the power of compounding interest. Or more specifically, the power of compounding the money he'd otherwise have given to the government, never to be seen again.

I met with Jonathan and Marcus at the same time.

We looked at how they could save on $100,000 of excess pre-tax income. They both perked up at the sound of that!

Jonathan would retain his $100,000 within his company, while Marcus would continue to receive all his income personally. Just to keep their different views on incorporating simple, we set aside various saving options like RSPs and just looked at the savings difference created by incorporating.

If Jonathan were to keep his extra $100,000 in his company, he'd pay only $11,000 on his $100,000 and have $89,000 left over to invest. Ten years later, at a 5% annual rate of return, his nest egg was projected to be a little over $1.1 million.

Since Marcus planned on receiving his $100,000 personally, what he received was after the government had taken a bite out of it. A big bite as it turns out. His $100,000 has now been reduced to $52,000. Ten years later and his nest egg is only $654,000.

A-ha you say … but remember, Jonathan will eventually pay tax to get his money out!

This is true, but while Marcus can look forward to very tax-efficient income, his portfolio will only produce $32,700 the following year, whereas Jonathan's would produce almost $56,000. That's a HUGE difference!

This is the power of incorporation—your ability to defer paying taxes. Your money works for you until you need it.

We've taken a look at the why, but how about the WHEN to incorporate?

Many of my clients tell me they were advised not to incorporate while they have debt. My answer to this is … it depends.

There are three reasons I say this to my clients.

1. If the thought of debt really makes you anxious, then let your heart lead and hammer your debt BEFORE you incorporate.

Yes, you'll pay a lot more in taxes to do so, but you'll feel secure a lot faster.

On the other hand, if you're like my wife and me, you may be comfortable with debt as long as it's strategic in nature. Let me show you what I mean.

Like many of us, my wife was raised to value being debt free while for me, being a business owner, I felt comfortable with keeping our mortgage for its duration and allowing my excess income we didn't need to grow within my company. Both of us were right, neither of us were wrong. Our views were both valid. What's important here is our values were heard and respected by the other.

We reached our compromise by ensuring we always had enough savings to pay off our mortgage if the sh*t hit the fan. This worked well until 2017, when the government announced its intention to implement their *Tax on Split Income* rule ("TOSI"). That same year my wife had chosen to leave her employment to start her own business, and she had a lower income that year.

I did an about-face.

We only had $65,000 left on our mortgage. It would only have cost us about $3,200 of interest over the remaining time to repay our mortgage, or $11,000 in taxes if I were to pay a dividend to my wife—enough to pay out our remaining mortgage.

Even though the numbers still showed we shouldn't pay it off early (i.e. the head), it was just too exciting to envision being debt-free (i.e. the heart.) So, we went for it and paid off our mortgage!

Remember. You're not locked into any decision, and you can adjust if your feelings on debt and savings change over time.

To this day however, I still get the stink eye from my accountant for paying off our mortgage early.

2. You may not become incorporated if where you run your practice won't pay into a corporate account.

For example, if you teach at a university, many universities won't pay into a corporation, which removes your ability to save in your company. There are other trade-offs however, such as more regular hours, benefits and often a pension plan. There's no right or wrong answer here, but it's just one more reason your planning should reflect your situation rather than a one-size-fits-all approach.

3. You have more than $50,000 per year in excess of what you need for daily living.

By keeping $50,000 in your company rather than receiving it personally, you can have up to $18,500 you would have given to the government now growing for you instead. Even once you factor in your set up and ongoing legal and accounting fees, that's some serious change you're keeping.

4. Another benefit of being incorporated is what's known as income-splitting.

Many of my clients have a lower income partner submitting their billings, which can be an effective way to split some of your income into their hands, as they'll be taxed at a much lower rate than yours. If they have little or no other income, you can save thousands in taxes. (How much you pay for the work done is best discussed with your accountant, lest you incur the ire of the Canada Revenue Agency.)

Oh, and don't forget to get a bookkeeper. Your value is in seeing patients, not chasing receipts. Save yourself a lot of time and aggravation and have your bookkeeper gift-wrap your information to your accountant.

So, if you find yourself comfortable with:

» your debt repayment plan (or have no debt—congratulations!)

» self-employment

» an extra $50,000 or more you can set aside for tomorrow

I want you to be incorporated.

———•———

A Head versus Heart Strategy To Use In Your Incorporation

Do you have a partner who is salary employed? If so, there's a risk of a power imbalance becoming a point of contention. Here's what I mean.

My wife and I had a head versus heart decision to make.

I mentioned my wife is a professional. When we had our mortgage, she was on a salary and bonus plan. Other than contributing to her RSP, she had no opportunity to defer taxes on any of her income.

And her income was in excess of what we needed as a family to run our household.

The question arose: did we need to take any money out of my company, when we could save more by only paying the lower corporate tax rate?

The head told us to use all her income toward our mortgage, lifestyle, and personal savings (RSPs and TFSAs), while I would 'top up' from my company only if we needed more. This would allow us to minimize our household income tax by my paying only 11% since we couldn't lower her tax rate.

The heart, however, said, "Wait a minute—we're using MY income while YOU get to save?" This strategy can create an unintended power imbalance. I never wanted my wife to feel she wasn't able to save while I could, even though the savings were really both of ours.

So how did we balance this head versus heart opportunity?

I became an employee of my own company, and put myself on salary. This had a couple of benefits. First, we could more equally contribute to our personal savings lifestyle and mortgage payments. No power imbalance.

Since realistically I'll never be in the lowest tax rates (and this is also true for pretty much all of my clients!), this allows me to use up my lower tax rates every year as I won't be able to get my savings out cheaper in the future anyway.

My wife and I both feel this is the best strategy.

AND HERE'S A QUESTION to think about: Do you think taxes are going to be higher or lower in the future? If you think they'll be higher, my guess is you're likely right. If so, you may want to pay a lower tax rate today over a higher rate tomorrow, at least until you get into our high tax rates.

To help avoid a power imbalance, soak up their lower tax rates, and have less income at the mercy of future tax-hungry governments, I like to see my incorporated clients pay themselves at least $100,000. (More of course, if your personal needs require it.)

How do you get incorporated?

Step 1: Get a proper financial plan created, so you can see if it makes sense to incorporate for YOUR unique values and situation. Your advisor should reach out to your accountant to discuss your plan, and see if they agree, or if there are other factors where they'd recommend delaying incorporation.

Step 2: Get your lawyer to apply to open your Professional Corporation with your College. Yes, you can do this yourself. But don't do it. Not only will your lawyer ensure things are completed right the first time, but remember your value is working with your patients not filling out forms!

Step 3: Once your Professional Corporation is approved, open a Corporate Bank account with your bank.

Step 4: Change your billings to reflect your Professional Corporation and bank account

Step 5: Work with your advisor and your accountant to determine how much of an income is best to pay yourself, keeping the rest of your income away from high personal tax rates!

And then rejoice in having kept more money in your company's pockets than the government's!

Chapter Summary Lessons:

1. Incorporation makes a lot of sense, but it's the timing that's often in question.

2. Money in your Professional Corporation goes a lot further than money given to the government.

3. Recognize the potential for compromise for balancing income with your partner.

Principle Three: Pay It Down

There are better ways to manage your debt.

CHAPTER 5

The Debt Dilemma

THINK OF HOW MUCH YOU BILL in a month.

Now, think about what you paid for your first car.

Put these two numbers beside each other, and you may see what I've found is the number one reason many doctors find themselves with too much debt.

Do you see the problem?

If you're like almost all of the doctors I've worked with, you stated your billings in pre-tax income, while the cost of your car was stated without tax you had to pay first.

The math doesn't add up, Doc.

Meet Peter. A Doctor With Buyer's Remorse.

Peter was one such doctor I've worked with. He earned about $300,000 a year as a family doctor, and had purchased a $80,000 car, and now he had wicked buyer's remorse every time he saw the monthly payment go out.

Here's the issue.

After taxes, Peter's income wasn't $300,000 … it was $195,000. Or about $16,250 per month. With a $10,000 per month lifestyle and a $4,000 per month mortgage, his car loan ate up all that was left.

"I thought that once I was in practice, things would be so much easier but I still feel like I'm just getting by." Peter said to me.

"Peter, I'm so glad we've met. Let's get out of this debt trap and get you some breathing room." I replied.

When his mortgage was up for renewal, we added his higher-interest car loan into his mortgage which freed up a lot of monthly cash.

Yes, over the life of the mortgage he'd pay more interest. But in Peter's head versus heart battle, it was really bothering him that he felt he lived month to month and couldn't save. Now he could.

I love helping doctors get out from their debt.

Early on in my business I drove to an event to speak for a study group of newly practicing doctors. While I have spoken often over the years, I was excited about this talk.

Rather than some prepared presentation, it was a candid opportunity for the doctors to ask me the financial questions burning in their minds. I love helping to increase my clients' financial understanding; it lets them ask better and better questions.

I was ready for anything they threw at me.

At first, the questions were the usual ones I get asked, such as when to incorporate or if rental properties are a good idea.

But the dam burst when one doctor asked me, "How do I know how much of a home I SHOULD buy? Everyone keeps telling me what I can afford, but I don't want to be working just to pay my mortgage."

This was such a great question. And it opened the flood gates!

"Is it better to lease or finance a car?"

"Should I rent first, or get a mortgage right away?"

"How fast should I repay my student loan?"

I could have been there all night.

All the questions were about debt.

There's what I often refer to as the debt dilemma, when a doctor is finally about to start building their practice.

The debt dilemma is this:

A newly practicing doctor can't wait to start attacking their student loans, while at the same time they're taking on more debt with a car loan or getting a mortgage.

Meanwhile, they're being advised to keep within lower tax rates by saving in their company, but they also see money disappear in interest for the loans that will now take longer to pay off.

Does this dilemma feel familiar?

If I asked you which debt you'd like to pay off first, what would you choose? If you're like most doctors I ask, you'd likely say, "The one with the highest interest rate!"

Thankfully, I don't believe in asking you that question.

Is paying off the debt with the highest interest rate truly what you really want, or is it the answer you think I want to hear from you?

I like to ask a much better question, which I'll share with you soon. Before we jump into that, consider why you might be asking:

"What debt should I repay first?"

The question doesn't work very well in the real world. Debt repayment isn't this black and white.

In fact, this common question asked of many financial advisors, which looks and sounds so normal, can be answered in many ways.

Here's the deal.

You can't really screw this up. You have three choices that all have pros and cons. You'll likely be somewhere in between. It all depends on what lets you sleep at night.

I want to help you understand what you're choosing between, so you can make the choice that feels the best.

You can follow your head, heart, or a combination of both.

Here is my favourite question to ask you about debt.

"When thinking of debt you'd like to get rid of, I'd like to know which of these is most important to you and why:

Freeing up cash flow, saving interest, or saving taxes?"

Why is erasing this debt important to you?

When I know WHY it's important to you, I'll also know you're much more likely to stay on track with a plan that reflects your why, and that leads to your financial success.

Let's look at your numbers AND your values. What are your views on debt, and where did they come from?

Was debt a concern when you were growing up? How your parents managed money can have a lasting impact on how you view debt as something to be avoided, ignored, or eliminated as quickly as possible.

Do you find debt tends to be a revolving door, where the moment you've paid it down it always seems to creep back up again? This can make you frustrated or ashamed and may cause you to procrastinate creating a plan that eliminates debt and helps you stay debt-free.

Or was debt never really an issue for you then or now? You see it as a strategic tool, rather than a necessary evil. If so, you probably focus on other goals over repaying debt quickly.

When you think of taking on new debt, how do you decide if it's a good idea or not?

The secret to creating a debt repayment plan is being able to STICK to your plan, and sleeping at night, comfortable with the time it will take to be debt free while achieving a balance with other goals—like growing your savings or enjoying a vacation. The value of stick-to-it-iveness (Yes—I made this word up) cannot be overstated!

For me, debt was never discussed when I was growing up, and yet it had to have been a factor for my parents who had a mortgage, furthered their education with Masters degrees, did a large home renovation and started a business.

An allowance of $5 per week seemed small to me then, but looking back I often wonder if it was generous since I didn't know if money was tight for them or not. I spent what I received, and waited until the next week if I used it too quickly. Debt just didn't exist for me then and it doesn't for most kids.

It wasn't until I was in university before I had my first experience with debt. My first credit card had a $500 limit … and like any good student with newfound freedoms, usually any available credit I saw as cash in my bank account. When my actual payday occurred, I'd pay down my credit card and then went back to using the credit card.

Nobody talked to me about interest rates, let alone how much work I had to do to have the money to pay 20% interest, (which was actually much higher when I factored in the taxes I had to pay before I could even pay my interest.) And that didn't even touch the outstanding balance owed.

It was fortunate I started to work as a part-time teller at a bank. Turns out, I loved understanding anything financial. It was the early 90s and I remember seeing mortgage rates of over 10%. I decided to look further into my own credit card and was shocked at what I was paying in interest, even if it appeared to be a small dollar amount.

I took it a step further and realized that I worked two full days just for the interest. I felt sick! That was the last time I ever carried a balance on my credit cards! For me, the joy of what I might use my credit card for was outweighed by the thought I'd have to work just to pay the interest.

I'm grateful I learned this lesson early on as a student.

Your Debt Can Be Used Creatively

You can use debt as a strategic tool; thoughtfully create a debt plan that helps you, and eliminate it while balanced against other goals you want to accomplish.

Do you think of debt as a useful tool, or does the thought of debt give you heart palpitations?

Are You Focusing On Debt To Avoid Investing?

Some doctors I've worked with over the years are okay with debt, but they distrust investments.

They tend to focus on debt elimination not because debt bothers them, but because they don't want to focus on a formalized investment plan. They don't feel comfortable with how their investments can go up and down in the market.

It's not a strategy I recommend.

The problem with this approach is you lose the ability of your savings to compound over time and ride out market fluctuations. Money's best friend is time.

Another issue that isn't so obvious is that you need time to acclimatize to the ups and down of the markets, so you don't react impulsively (and almost always negatively) when the markets drop.

Remember my client Chris, the doctor who did a great job in repaying his debt but was at risk of burning out? As it turns out, the reason he'd been so focused on repaying their debt wasn't only because he hated paying interest. In one of our meetings, he confessed: "Adrian. I'm coming clean. The main reason why I didn't invest is that I just didn't trust investments. I thought they were a gamble."

The thought of losing money to interest was one thing, but the thought of losing money in his savings *really* bothered him.

While being debt free was certainly something to celebrate, it also came with several problems:

1. **He had hemorrhaged tax.** For every extra dollar he took from his Professional Corporation to hammer his debt meant he had to cut a cheque to the CRA for almost the same amount as well. That's a whole new meaning to the phrase "stroke a cheque", and it was money he could have had growing for him instead.

2. **He lost his most valuable resource … time.** Markets rise, fall, and rise again. You may have heard it's time in the market, not market timing, that's the key to investment success and it's true. He'd lost ten years of being able to ride out and compound his gains.

3. **He had a big and difficult mountain to climb.** Chris must now save aggressively if he wants to retire on time. But it's more than that. If he didn't like volatility before, he certainly wasn't going to like it when one negative year in ten years has a much greater impact than over twenty years.

When I truly understood what had been Chris' actual motivation, it really helped shape the rest of our conversations. Remember, there's no right or wrong answer in most of your financial decisions.

What's important is to know beforehand what *you're giving up first*.

We'll cover more about this issue in a later chapter, but for now it's important to understand the push and pull battle between your head and your heart.

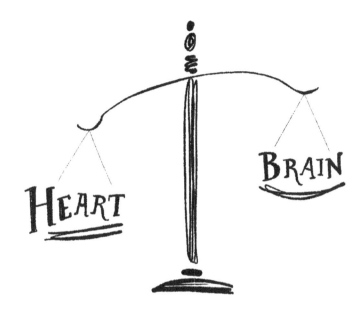

Your Head Says Be Logical About Debt

If you're incorporated, you look at the personal taxes you'd have to pay before you could put any additional money onto your loan or mortgage.

Here's a hard fact. In Alberta, at least a quarter of your income is gone in taxes before you do anything.

So, you might choose to pay less in taxes (11% small business tax in Alberta), and put the money you'd otherwise have given to the government toward growing your net worth instead.

That can be up to 37 cents more of every dollar you earn working for you!

Your Heart Says Pay Down The Loans

You also likely hate seeing your car or student loan payments every month. Sure, nobody likes paying more in tax, but you just can't help but think how great it will feel to be debt-free and not have to make those payments every month.

Maybe you'd rather ditch the loan first so the monthly payment will stop and THEN look to increasing your savings. You're okay that you've lost a little time for your money to grow, because now you feel you're saving from a rock-solid foundation.

Here's a game changer.

You don't need to choose.

Remember the Head and Heart Formula

You can build a custom-balanced plan based on the numbers that work for you AND what's based on your ability to sleep well at night!

While the exact mix between head and heart is personal to everyone, here is my **Head and Heart Formula**:

1. **Shorter repayment timelines (think car loans).** Pay these off aggressively to free up cash flow.

2. **Longer repayment timelines (think mortgages).** Don't pay these off aggressively unless you're really debt-adverse.

3. **Medium repayment timelines (think student loans).** This debt I often call "the intangibles". Your student loans created an extremely valuable asset—your ability to earn your income. But your knowledge isn't something you can easily sell to repay your debt if needed. If not having a physical asset tied to your loan is your greater concern, then attack this debt.

Head vs heart is one of the most important reasons your plan needs to be unique to you. You'll stick with it, make progress, and feel great about it!

It's rewarding to see one of your debts gone, and this creates great money habits as you then roll your payments from one retired debt to the next.

Let's dive into the different kinds of debt so you can start **creating your Head and Heart Formula.**

Debt Wears Many Hats

Debt isn't as cut and dried as you think.

You've probably heard the expression Good Debt vs Bad Debt.

But debt is much deeper, wider, and more flexible than that. Is a car loan 'bad' debt? We need cars to get to work and earn income, but what if that car is a very expensive one? Is it good debt or bad debt then?

A car is never really just a car.

I would encourage you to shift your thinking from good and bad debt to understanding constructive and consumption debt.

Constructive Debt Helps Your Net Worth Grow

Constructive debt comes in many forms, and is usually tied to something that grows or produces income, or both.

The home your mortgage purchased is one form of constructive debt that works to grow your net worth. Your student loan allows you to earn your income, even though it's not tied to a growing asset.

Both types of constructive debt accelerate your journey toward financial independence.

All those years of no-name canned soup were worth it!

Consumption Debt Decreases Your Net Worth

Consumption debt are those debts where there's little or no future value to what was purchased with it.

How many times have you been surprised by the size of your credit card bills, made up of a lot of little purchases? Or maybe you're still paying for that wonderful family vacation, months after it ended? These kinds of expenses build up debt that's carried over to the next month.

This is where addressing your money habits first will help you the most, instead of just paying down debt that comes back like a boomerang. Keep reading! I've got more on this in a later chapter.

Having fun and making memories is important—they make life worth living.

But remember this rule.

If it's something you're going to consume, like a much-needed family vacation, it's better to set up a savings plan toward that goal than to utilize debt to fund it. It's not that you should avoid debt, but rather I want you thinking strategically about it before taking it on.

We'll dig deeper into consumption debt after this chapter!

Constructive Debt (Tied To Assets): The 3 Basic Types

Is your debt tied to an asset? If so, what type?

Let's take a look at your debt that's tied to assets. In most cases, there are three types:

1. A lease or a loan for a vehicle, which usually depreciates in value.

2. A loan or a line of credit for your education—an asset but not a tangible one which could be sold if you found yourself unable to work.

3. A mortgage for a home, which usually appreciates in value.

Should you pay off a debt attached to a decreasing, increasing or intangible asset? It depends.

You need to ask these questions:

1. What is your actual interest rate anyway?

We live in a multiverse of tax rates:

» Pre-tax (your income or RSP savings)

» Lightly taxed (income you keep in your company after expenses and paying yourself)

» Deferred tax (investment growth isn't typically taxed until sold)

» After-tax (your living expenses, Registered Education Savings Plan and TFSA contributions for example)

2. How much of your after-tax income is needed to make your payments?

Car loans tend to be much higher payments, relative to their outstanding balance, due to the shorter repayment time frame (3-5 years) rather than a mortgage which is often twenty-five years to repay. On the other hand, because of the longer repayment time for your mortgage, paying more earlier means less for interest to compound over so many years.

3. Are you incorporated into a Professional Corporation ("PC")?

I talked earlier about how saving money in your PC and not spending more in personal income tax might appeal to you.

Or, if the thought of such a large debt keeps you awake at 2 a.m.?

Then maybe taxes aren't the bigger drivers for you.

Don't worry. You can keep both your head and heart happy!

Meet Anuka and Vikram. Juggling Debt Repayment.

Many newly practicing doctors find themselves in a situation like what I encountered with Vik and Anuka. They had:

1. An average personal tax rate of 36%.

2. Both were incorporated into Professional Corporations.

3. Their debt consisted of:

    a. A 5-year car loan for $50,000, with payments of $850 per month at only 0.4% interest.

    b. Combined student loans and lines of credit for another $250,000 that had them paying $3,000 per month at a 6% interest rate, and

    c. A new $750,000 mortgage with $4,400 per month payments at 5% interest.

They were conflicted in what to do now they were finally both out and working.

Option A: I Want More Monthly Cash Flow

Vik and Anuka could pay off their car loan much faster than their student loans or mortgage. This wouldn't save them much in interest, but BOY it would sure feel great to have one less payment to make and they could see it happening within the year.

Once their car payment was eliminated, they could add that payment amount to accelerating their student loan repayments.

This is what Vik wanted.

Just seeing one less payment would give him peace of mind. It would also allow him to feel more relaxed about starting his investments, as he wouldn't feel he had made a 'wrong' decision if the markets were to drop.

Option B: I Hate Losing Money to Interest

Anuka hates paying interest.

Working as hard as she did to get through residency, it really upsets her to see her income leaking away every month just to pay interest.

Growing her investment portfolio is one thing, but Anuka also feels she'd prefer a known savings (the interest she'd otherwise have to pay) over a possible gain which can go up and down.

For Anuka, whether she hates interest or distrusts the markets (or both!)—paying her highest after-tax interest rate gives her a sense of secure savings.

Anuka hated seeing her student loans increase.

For Anuka, she wanted to see this debt gone first.

Paying off this intangible debt would give her the most peace of mind.

However, it did bother both Vik and Anuka that they wouldn't be adding to their savings.

Option C: I Want to Get Rid of My Debt AND Save

Maybe you want to use your money both ways—get rid of your debt while also saving.

If this appeals to you, start here instead:

Determine how much extra you can pay yourself *above* what you currently need while staying in the same tax bracket. The extra money in your company above that amount you can put toward your corporate savings.

This is how we solved the dilemma for Vik and Anuka.

Anuka and Vik's 5-Year Debt Crusher Plan:

They were each paying themselves $120,000 per year, which put them at the 36% tax rate. They would jump to just over 41% tax rate at $165,000 of income.

So, here's an unusual strategy I recommend to my clients in this position. They could pay themselves each $45,000 *more than they were* while staying in the same tax bracket.

We took that extra amount of personal income and stomped down their car loan.

With their remaining income we saved in their Prof Corps, we first set up an emergency savings account which allowed Anuka to feel secure. If needed, they'd have the money to wipe out their student loans while they first focused on freeing up cash flow.

It would take ten months to pay off their car loan, at which point we'd switch the combined payments to attacking their student loans. That would be just under four more years.

This 5-year plan to eliminate their debt meant they'd free up cash flow (appealing to Vik), have emergency savings (appealing to Anuka), and be debt free (excluding their mortgage) within five years.

Of course, you might feel you just want to pay off as much of your debt as you can each year regardless of taxes. A number of my clients feel this way.

But my recommendation is to take a year or two longer and pay a much lower amount of tax than the interest you'd save. Keep the difference in your Professional Corporation and see your savings grow as your debt shrinks.

While this balance doesn't fully tackle your debt or fully grow your savings, it does allow you to feel good about seeing an end in sight for your debt while also seeing your savings grow.

And a good portion of that growth is the taxes you would otherwise have given to the government!

Growing your net worth faster (head), or paying off debt and having a more stable foundation (heart)—both are great options.

What option do most of my doctor clients choose?

In my experience of working with many doctors over so many years, rarely do they focus on the interest rate. Ironically, despite that, they will still usually tell me they want the option that has them paying the least amount of interest.

But when I ask, "I'd like to know what's most important to you, and if you could tell me why: freeing up cash flow, saving interest, or saving taxes?", they usually sit for a moment and go quiet.

It's not a question they expected.

Something interesting happens *after* I ask my clients to answer my **Head vs Heart** questions.

Once they realize they have other creative options AND are liberated from the feeling of making a 'wrong' decision, they almost immediately release their worries about paying interest.

Most of the doctors I work with tell me they want to free up cash flow with faster-to-repay debt elimination and THEN switch to saving taxes by focusing on savings (and leaving their mortgages alone).

Once your first debt has been eliminated, you'll be in a better position to decide if you want to keep attacking debt, or grow your savings more with the money you were putting on that debt.

Once you see progress? You'll feel more secure in both your work and your ability to save. Remember, there's no right or wrong answer here, and paying off a debt is both a reason to celebrate and also for you to take stock to see if you want to adjust your plan.

Your debt shouldn't feel like a weight on your back.

Debt doesn't have to be an unmanageable weight. You have debt repayment options that can make life feel lighter and move you successfully to your goals.

So, let's go back to my question.

What's most important to you—head or heart?

Take a moment and visualize your smallest debt being paid off first.

Now visualize the amount of interest saved if you tackled your debt with the highest interest rate.

Were you most excited for one less payment to make or freeing up cash flow by paying off your lowest balance first?

If the thought of saving interest was most exciting, then a plan to eliminate your highest interest debt should be discussed.

Not sure which option is most exciting for you?

You may want to do both by using Option C. It allows you to withdraw a planned amount from your company to apply to your personal debt until you hit the higher tax rates, and saving the rest in your company.

Remember, there's really no wrong answer here.

———•———

And I know you may be worried about something.

"Adrian, what if I change my mind and want to switch options?"

Breathe.

While you should stick with your planning, you can also change your mind and plan if life unfolds differently—you're never locked in.

Between saving interest, saving taxes, or freeing up cash flow? I admit I like one less payment to have to make. Proper planning will help you decide which matters most to you.

There's always a way to keep both your head and heart happy!

———•———

Chapter Summary Lessons:

1. Understand your views on debt, and how your partner's views may differ.

2. Reframe your debt question to one that makes sense—what bothers you most about it?

3. Is your debt helping you build your net worth, or reducing it?

CHAPTER 6

How Much Home Should You Own?

BUYING A HOME STIRS UP A mix of emotions. You think you'll be logical and patient.

But once you start looking? Forget it!

You'll be surprised at how quickly you'll buy a home when your plan was to wait a year or two. In fact, it happens so quickly that when I hear a client tell me they're 'just looking", I know what they're really saying is,

"We've found our dream home and we need to line up financing right away!"

When my wife and I looked for a home, we had the usual questions.

Was it close to a good school? Did it have nearby parks? Was it a safe and quiet neighborhood? How much of a down payment would we need, and what would it cost to furnish our house the way we wanted it?

Having been a former loans officer, I knew we had great credit and qualified for a mortgage. We shopped for the best rate, decided if we wanted a fixed or variable rate, and provided our down payment. Everywhere we looked, we were told how much of a mortgage we would qualify for.

We had done as most of us do; we found the home we wanted, ensured we could afford the mortgage payments, and proceeded to buy our home.

Years later, now that I'm an experienced home buyer, I know we weren't asked this question:

How much of a home SHOULD we look for?

Here are three questions we should have been asked:

1. How much of a down payment did we want, in order to find a balance between lower mortgage payments against other growth opportunities?

2. Did we see this being our permanent home? If so, would we want to do any future renovations?

3. Did we see our jobs changing in the future?

Our focus at the time, other than finding the right neighborhood, was simply to avoid paying any Canadian Housing and Mortgage Company (CMHC) fees. What's that you may ask?

In Canada, to protect our financial system and keep it healthy, banks are required to have your mortgage insured from default by a company such as CMHC when you have less than 20% of the purchase price as a down payment.

If for some reason you were unable to make your payments and the bank needed to use their *Power to Sell* clause in your mortgage agreement *and* there wasn't enough after the sale to fully pay off your mortgage? Then CMHC would step in to cover the difference. This keeps banks happy to lend to qualified borrowers.

Depending on how much of a down payment you have, the fees can be between 2.4% and 4% of your purchase price. So, if you wanted to buy a $700,000 home and had less than $140,000 (20%) as a down payment—you'd have a $16,800 -$28,000 fee added into your mortgage.

Yikes!

But is that necessarily a bad thing? Let me explain.

What if you found the perfect home for the perfect price, but waiting until you had your 20% down payment meant the price moved up *more* than your CMHC fee would be for buying it now, or worse, someone else ended up buying the house?

I'm not trying to give you license to buy on a whim, but I also want you to remember:

Don't let the CHMC-fee-tail wag the dog.

Get me involved, and do it right when you're first thinking about a new home. Let's make sure your home fits your plan vs trying to squeeze your plan into the wrong home.

———•———

Meet Ali: To Buy or To Wait?

Ali, one of my clients, was looking to buy a home, but felt unsure as she didn't have the 20% down payment for what she thought was her target price range.

It also caused her to wonder if she should bother getting incorporated, since she "was just going to take it out anyway for the down payment."

Thank goodness we met beforehand, not afterward. There were several things we accomplished because we met and planned her home purchase early.

First, we determined how much she wanted to spend per month that felt comfortable for her. That allowed Ali to go forward knowing she wouldn't have buyer's remorse for buying too much of a house. No one wants to be house-poor and own a fancy house with beat-up college furniture inside. Second, when she met with my mortgage broker (he's amazing!), she wasn't only able to line up a favourable pre-approval rate, but he also steered her away from lenders who do sneaky things like advertise the lowest rates, but compound monthly (industry standard is to compound every six months in arrears). That was like adding .25% to her mortgage rates if he hadn't dug in to find her the best VALUE mortgage.

Third, while we PLANNED that she could buy a home in a couple of years, Ali was READY to buy a home if it was the right house for the right price, even if she didn't have the full 20% down payment yet.

Planning early for the amount of home you SHOULD buy is far better than trying to figure out how to pay for the home you were told you COULD buy.

Should you use a mortgage broker or your bank's lender?

In my experience, it's hard to beat going with a mortgage broker.

Some banks only use their own staff, but most brokers can shop the market. They're usually able to negotiate better deals because they bring a lot of business to a favourite lender. *And it doesn't cost you a dime more than it would if you used your own bank.*

One of my clients, Anthony, was recommended by his accountant to use a bank's personal banker for a construction mortgage. A construction mortgage is often used when building a new home, and they lend the funds out in stages as portions of the build are completed.

The problem for Anthony was the bank wanted a large down payment while also wanting other loans paid off ahead of time like his student loan. There was just no way for Anthony to do both at the same time.

In came my mortgage broker, who not only shopped the market to find a better rate, but also a mortgage where my client would need to have the down payment by the END of the build, not BEFORE it could start. Since the build was scheduled to take two years, this gave Anthony plenty of time to pay off some of his debts while getting the down payment ready.

Anthony was relieved and thrilled!

So why was the banker recommended? Turns out, they had a reciprocal agreement with the accountant to refer clients to each other. Thankfully, Anthony had gone with my broker instead, avoiding a delay in building their house and before the property was sold to someone else.

My recommendation is to see what your bank can offer, and provide that information to your mortgage broker and let them compete. You'll win not only on the best rate, but you'll often have the most flexibility as well.

So how to best save for your down payment?

You have lots of options.

Knowing what you need to save is the first step, and remember your down payment savings are likely going to be needed within the next few years.

Do NOT invest them into anything that isn't guaranteed. Heck, just a high interest savings account would be ideal.

3 vehicles to help you save effectively:

1. First Time Home Buyers' Incentive (FTHBIs)

If you have at least 5% of your purchase price for a down payment, the government gives you 5-10% (matching) if your income is below $120,000. If you live in Vancouver, Toronto or Montreal, this income cap is increased to $150,000. So, this may be of interest to investigate before you start working, but there is a catch. The government owns their proportional equity alongside you and when you sell, they get their proportionate amount back. If you gain, so do they (but if your home loses in value, they share that as well).

This option can be great for residents, but not once you start practicing and earning more.

2. Tax-Free First Home Savings Account (FHSAs)

In the 2022 Federal Budget: if you're a resident of Canada over the age of 18 who hasn't owned a home in the current or previous four years (and yes, that includes if your spouse or partner had one during that time), you can participate in the new FHSA plans. Your contributions are deductible from your taxable income.

You can contribute up to $40,000 each, with a yearly limit of $8,000. This can save you between $2,000 – $4,000 each per year, so planning early for your home will help you maximize this over the 5 years needed to hit your $40,000. You can make your contribution and use it as a deduction against the current or future year's income—very handy if you plan on being in a higher tax bracket later!

Growth isn't taxed, and neither are your withdrawals if they are used to purchase your home.

This is a big win for home buyers.

3. Home Buyers' Plan (HBP)

Another way you can save is by contributing up to $35,000 each into your *Registered Retirement Savings Plan* (RRSP), if you have the allowable contribution room. When you look to purchase a home and provide a closing agreement showing the amount of down payment needed within 90 days (it must be your principal residence and not a rental or vacation property,) you can withdraw $35,000 each.

Starting the second year after withdrawal, you need to repay at least $1/15^{th}$ each year over the next 15 years. Any amount of that $1/15^{th}$ not repaid is considered taxable income in that year (and sorry—you don't get a 2nd tax deduction for repaying.)

For example, if you borrowed $30,000 from your RSP this year (year 1), you wouldn't need to start your repayments until the year after next (year 3). In that 3rd year, you'd have to repay at least $2,000 $(1/15^{th})$ to your RSP. If you only repaid $1,000 that year however, you'd have to pay tax on the remaining $1,000 you didn't repay.

I've seen 'advice' that this hurts the growth of your RSP, and maybe it does. But they neglect to mention how that money is now in your home which itself tends to grow in value.

Homebuyer Withdrawal Plans allow you to take a lump sum out, while evening out your repayments to stay in a lower tax bracket.

#1: **IF YOU ALREADY** have over $35,000 in your RSP, consider opening a Spousal RSP if you can. Doing so lets you use your contribution room to deposit into your spouse or partner's plan, even if they had no earned income. Then you can both withdraw $35,000 from your respective plans to help buy your home.

#2: **IT MAY MAKE** sense NOT to repay the 1/15th if your spouse or partner have little or no taxable income that year. Instead, consider putting that repayment toward their TFSA. You save on the taxes going in, pay little or no on the way out, and turn around and grow it tax-free instead!

Tax Free Savings Accounts (TFSAs)

TFSAs started in 2009 and allow money you deposit into your TFSA to grow tax-free, and can be withdrawn tax-free later. The catch? You must use after-tax personal dollars to contribute.

There are two big bonuses with TFSAs (besides no tax):

1. Unlike RSPs that require earned income (such as salary, not dividends, from your company) to create contribution room; for TFSAs you simply have to be the age of majority in your province. So, if one of you isn't working, or you didn't have much in the way of earned income while in school, you still can have up to $88,000 contribution room each (assuming you were an adult in 2009 when they were first launched.) This number can be found on your *Notice of Assessment* you receive when you file your taxes.

2. When you take out your savings from your TFSA, you gain that amount of contribution room for future deposits, *starting the next year.* That last point is very important— taking savings out and recontributing some or all the same year, IF you don't have additional contribution room that

year, can result in a 1% penalty per month until you withdraw the excess.

Which option feels the best for your situation?

Let's put this all together.

You and your partner want to buy a $900,000 home, and you'd like to avoid paying CMHC fees if at all possible. So, you set out to save $180,000 (20%) for your down payment.

Here's how that might look:

Step 1: Open a First Home Savings Account, and each person contributes $8,000 and deducts it from their taxable income (if you're in a higher tax rate, otherwise deduct it in a later year when you are!)

Achievement: $80,000 put away over the next five years, and up to $38,400 in taxes saved.

Step 2: Open a RSP (or Spousal RSP if one partner is in a low or no tax bracket) and plan on contributing up to $35,000 each. You'll get a deduction also, so plan accordingly to ensure you're deducting your contributions advantageously against your income tax!

Achievement: $70,000 more put away, with $150,000 total savings.

Step 3: Open a Tax-Free Savings Account (TFSA) for any remaining amount of savings (in this case, $40,000) IF you have excess personal income. If you're incorporated however, it may be best to simply save in your company and take out what you need when you need it to top up your down payment if you're already in a high tax bracket.

Being A Doctor Pays In More Ways Than One!

You'll find banks trip over themselves to lend to doctors.

Many banks we work with have a loan specially designed for doctors for up to 10% of the purchase price for your down payment. While this means you would borrow up to 90%, you could avoid the CMHC fees.

Different rules apply if your home price is over $1,000,000—so you need to do the planning early.

Yes—that's where I come in.

You can become mortgage free fastest by NOT paying it off early.

That caught your attention!

Listen, I know you want to pay your mortgage off early. But what no one tells you is that when you're an incorporated doctor? *Paying down your mortgage faster isn't necessarily in your best interest.*

I can tell you just raised your eyebrows.

What would happen if you were to take the high monthly amount you'd pay for a 10-year mortgage, but instead go with a lower monthly payment, 25-year mortgage and save the difference?

Get ready to be blown away.

Let's say you have a $500,000 mortgage at 5%. Your payments would be $2,900 per month over the next twenty-five years as you pay $372,000 of interest. But if you wanted to go aggressively and pay it back in ten years, your payments almost double to $5,300 per month and you'll have paid about $135,000 of interest—which saves you $237,000.

Not bad!

But you'd pay more in tax than you would save in interest. Whattttttt??

I know. It's shocking.

What if you had decided to keep the extra $2,400 per month you were putting on your mortgage, and instead saved it within your Prof Corp?

If this amount only had your small business rate applied, you could have as much as $4,100 per month to add to your savings. Seven years later at a 5% yearly return, while your mortgage would be around $415,000, your investments in your PC would be over $420,000.

Congratulations, you're debt-free!

Well, not *technically* since you still owe the bank $415,000 on your mortgage. But you'd have $420,000 in your Prof Corp investments *that are growing faster than your decreasing interest payments of your mortgage as you continue to repay it.*

I really love the nerdy numbers!

Look at what happens the following year for your savings against your mortgage interest:

Your investment portfolio of $420,000 would grow by $21,000 (if at 5%), and your remaining $415,000 mortgage would have interest over the next year of about $20,750 (if still at 5% interest.)

This gap continues to widen every year after, and growing your net worth!

One more thing I love about this strategy. Should the sh*t hit the fan, you have the money to continue to pay your mortgage, or even eliminate it altogether, in the event of a disability or an interruption in your ability to work.

Paying off your mortgage early has two problems:

1. The money you pay in tax could have gone toward growing your wealth.

2. Paying off your mortgage early has a diminishing return.

If you paid off your mortgage tomorrow, you'd save a finite amount of interest. By that I mean the money you used to pay off your mortgage doesn't continue to save you interest, and the growth of your home is unaffected whether or not you have a mortgage attached to it.

But if you put that cash into growing your savings within investments, there isn't a cap on what your money can grow to. Yes, stocks go up and down, BUT the money is in YOUR pocket, not the government's nor the bank's. And historically the stock market has continued to grow through all sorts of market turbulence.

Does this mean you should always just go with the longest length of mortgage? Absolutely not. One of my clients absolutely hates debt and didn't care about the taxes he had to pay in order to hammer his mortgage. Only a few years later, he's debt free and very securely building his wealth.

There is no right or wrong answer when it comes to head versus heart decisions about your wealth.

What's important is that you ask yourself the right questions about what you really want (or to avoid), and have your planning reflect it.

How much of a down payment, who to get it from, and how to repay it against your other options are just a few of the reasons it's so important for you to have a STRATEGIC plan for your debt, especially *before* you take it on.

Plan well, plan early. (I sound like my dad!)

Chapter Summary Lessons:

1. You can be debt-free faster by not repaying debt faster, and be better protected as well.

2. Plan for your home purchase early, but don't let the CMHC-tail wag the dog.

3. Use a broker to compete with your banker for your best mortgage.

4. You can only save so much interest, but your savings have no limit to their growth.

Principle Four: Protect It

You've worked hard for your income.
Now let's make it bullet-proof.

Insurance Is All About Perspective

I'LL NEVER FORGET THE FIRST TIME I purchased life insurance. My wife and I had just bought our home with a $543,000 mortgage. I wasn't insurance licensed at the time, but I did the quick math that getting a $500,000 term 20 (meaning the premiums would stay the same for 20 years) life insurance policy on both me and my wife would cover our needs. I never gave much thought to anything else like: should we include our plans to have children, would we need insurance once they were grown or our mortgage was paid off, or how it could be used to secure our retirement and our eventual estate.

I did what many people do. I used the *This-Equals-That* formula and thought,

"Well, this is easy."

We called an insurance company, and an agent came over and went through pages after pages of health questions. Not once did he ask a question about our future goals. Worse yet, he kept talking about himself! He wanted to get in and out quickly, and honestly, we wanted him to leave as quickly as he did.

Two hours later, $55 per month for me, and $35 per month for my wife; we had our policies in place and went about our lives.

We didn't realize we'd just been taken through the McInsurance drive-thru.

We quickly found our insurance needs were much greater than what we were sold, as our careers and our family grew. The insurance agent who spoke with my wife and me had missed the boat completely.

Insurance Isn't Add Water And Stir

There were so many things that, in hindsight, should have been discussed. What benefits did either of our jobs offer? What were our current and future needs? How much coverage should we have obtained, and what type of insurance did we need?

I started creating our own financial plan. (You'd be surprised how few financial planners have done a plan for their own family!) As I got deeper into our planning, it became increasingly clear we were not only significantly underinsured, but we had gaps of no protection at all.

It wasn't just that we didn't have any additional life insurance to replace our income if one of us were to pass away. If one of us developed cancer, both of our incomes would have been affected.

The one who was sick, and the other who would have to reduce their work to help with the care and our children.

Not only that, I had absolutely no protection should a disability impact my ability to earn a living.

Suddenly our $500,000 term life insurance policies seemed woefully inadequate.

There were so many questions which, in hindsight, should have been discussed. What benefits did either of our jobs offer? What were our current and future needs? How much coverage should we have obtained, and what types of insurance did we need?

I knew I needed to become insurance licensed to ensure my family and my clients were properly advised and protected. It was one of the best things I've ever done.

I never wanted to have to say to my clients, or worse, their families, that I was sorry they weren't properly protected and now they had some major financial and lifestyle decisions to make. Why? They didn't have enough money to cover their needs.

Imagine your partner or spouse hearing those words.

Imagine someone saying those words to YOU.

The need to help my clients before a health event became the driving force in my career.

Instead of insurance being the last after-thought component of your financial plan—it's now one of the first things I talk to my clients about. Once you have your protection in place, we have the luxury of time to determine your preferred debt and savings goals, knowing the income to support your plan is secure.

I get it. No one wants to talk about the possibility of early death or disability. It freaks many people out. However, you're in the medical field and you know better than most how quickly things can happen.

I don't want you to make the same mistake my wife and I did. Fortunately, we were able to get our proper protection in place. And I no longer think of it as some pain-in-the-ass thing I need to pay for.

Here's a quirky fact you need to know about insurance:

You buy insurance with your health, not your wealth. Yes—you read that right.

Once your health has changed, insurance can become more expensive, have exclusions, or worse—you might not be able to get it at all.

In my younger years, I felt like I was beating the system by not having paid to protect my income. Now viewed through the lens of decades of experience, I realize I'd simply been very lucky nothing had happened.

So that insurance you've been dragging your feet over?

Get your proper protection in place. Do it today. I kid you not.

How To Create The Insurance Protection You Need

I want to help you find the balance between getting the right type and amount of insurance, while also making sure you don't buy too much.

Why pay for what you don't need?

Do you remember the first time someone proposed insurance to you? Most likely you heard about all the odds and statistics for becoming disabled, and how all manner of ailments were right around the corner.

And once you met with the salesperson, they started in on everything they could sell you. I don't know about you, but I don't like to see dollar signs flashing in the salesperson's eyes.

So, how can you determine the amount and type of insurance YOU need?

Let's back up for a second.

I want you to think about receiving two job offers. They're identical in every way, from city to type of practice, hours, etc., but the first offer pays you $400,000 per year and the 2nd pays you $390,000.

Based on ONLY that information, which offer would you accept?

You're probably thinking, "Wait a second. There's more to this.", and you're right, there is. But for now, it's probably safe to assume you'd be like most people and pick the first offer that pays you more.

Let's go a little deeper.

The first job offer would pay you nothing if you became disabled, while the second job offer would pay you $8,500 per month tax-free.

The first job offer would pay you nothing if you should suffer a heart attack, stroke, or develop cancer. The second job offer would pay you $500,000—again tax-free.

Should you prematurely pass away, the first job offer would pay nothing to those who depend upon your income. The second job offer would provide $3,500,000 tax-free to keep them financially stable.

Now if you were presented with $400,000 with no benefits, or $390,000 with protection for you and your family should you become disabled, become critically ill or prematurely pass away— which would you choose?

Why do we tend to quickly switch in favour of the $390,000 offer when presented this information?

Having to separately purchase insurance in the first offer can feel like a necessary evil. But with the second offer it feels like you get so much more value.

This is how I want you to think about your own insurance needs.

Your "true" income is lower, but you "get" all these other benefits. It also helps to move you away from odds and statistics, and to feel liberated to allocate your $390,000 as you want to.

A Strange Question About Insurance Premiums

I know it's unconventional, but I get my clients to look at their premiums from a different angle. Before we look at any kind of insurance options, we look at your money in a new light:

Where else could you put that insurance premium?

Let's assume I've recommended a protection portfolio with premiums of $500 per month for your disability, critical illness, and life insurance needs. How might you benefit if you allocated that $500 per month to something else?

Let's analyze this $500 per month—$6,000 per year— chunk of cash.

If you have debt, such as a mortgage, we can calculate your additional interest savings. On a $500,000 mortgage at 4% over twenty-five years, that extra $500 per month would save you about $80,000 of interest over the life of your mortgage.

What if you saved the $500 per month instead? Over twenty years it would add up to an additional $205,000 of savings—not bad!

But now, let me ask you one question: which of the following will have the most IMPACT to your ability to become financially independent?

1. $80,000 of interest saved

2. $205,000 of additional investments

3. Losing a year or more of your income if you or your partner had a health event.

I know this seems like a loaded question, but it's important to know what you're truly choosing between.

Hey, I'm not here to ensure you're wealthy. You're doing that heavy lifting already!

I'm here to ensure you're never poor.

The Three Insurance Types: Disability, Critical Illness, and Life Insurance.

Do you need them all? It depends.

Here's a quick breakdown for you (we'll dive a little deeper later):

Disability Protection:

At its most basic level, a disability is a physical or mental condition that limits or prevents your ability to work. This can be temporary such as a broken wrist, or a longer or even potentially permanent concern such as depression or anxiety. Disability protection has the largest spectrum of possible conditions and because of which, is the most likely to occur during your working years.

Critical Illness:

If you should suffer a life-threatening illness such as cancer, critical illness is designed to come in as a lump-sum to allow you to focus on your health, not your finances.

In addition to the obvious drop in your income, if you have a working spouse or partner it's likely their ability to work full time is going to be impacted. There are also a host of unanticipated additional expenses if you're sick. Critical illness helps to fill these financial gaps.

Life Insurance: The Big D

Usually, this one needs very little explanation, but while it's the least likely of the three to occur during your working career, it's the only one that is 100% certain to happen at some point. The big question of course, is when?

Life insurance has so many uses, but protecting future income is one of the most important.

Your family and others you care about who rely on you are the biggest reasons you need to get it. It transfers risk from those who would be financially devastated to an insurance company who can absorb it.

So, let's take that deeper dive into these three, so you can see what type, amount, and features are the most appropriate for YOUR unique situation.

Another reason why I choose to work with doctors?

I hate seeing you sold high-premium permanent life insurance when I know you have other things you need to worry about.

You're focused on buying your home, paying off your debt, saving for your children's education, or going on a well-deserved vacation to keep from burnout.

What you don't need is to worry about what your estate tax will be sixty years from now. I've not met anyone early in their career who is worried about "funeral and final expenses", but I encounter doctors all the time where someone has sold them those kinds of policies as well.

Getting you protected with inexpensive term insurance so you're covered while you accomplish your goals allows me to achieve MY goal of making them happen.

For me, it's not just a race against time to get you protected before a health event occurs, but also a race to secure you before you've wasted thousands on policies that don't fit with your current goals.

I'm the Doctors-Get-Your-Act-Together-Whisperer.

Chapter Summary Lessons:

1. Get your insurance today. You'll have lower premiums and the health to get it with.

2. It's better to plan with 100% certainty on 95% of your income, than 0% certainty on 100% of it.

3. It's more important to get term coverage for the amount you need, over a lower permanent coverage for something decades away.

CHAPTER 8

Why You Need Life Insurance

LIFE INSURANCE IS ONE OF THOSE quirky parts of your financial planning.

Why? You have to face the future-dead-you.

You know you will die one day.

But dying is a tough concept to absorb when you're living your life, working, dropping the kids off to daycare, taking the dog for a walk, and hitting the drive-thru for your coffee on the way to work.

Death is always something that will happen, just not today, so you tend to put off getting proper life insurance coverage to some day in the future.

Ironically, if you knew today WAS the day, you couldn't get life insurance no matter how much you were willing to pay for it.

———•———

Here's what I know to be true for me:

I'm only going to die once, and I'm sure not going to do it for free.

Kidding aside, life insurance allows me to plan my vision and dreams for my family's future; and that my loved ones can stay in our family home. Having life insurance also means I can look forward to maximizing our retirement spending, with a tax-free estate that keeps the tax collector's hands off of what our kids receive.

There's another reason you'll be happy to have the right insurance in place.

When you're no longer alive to enjoy what you've worked hard to build, there's only three places your money can go:

1. Your family and your friends

2. Your community and your charity

3. The Canada Revenue Agency (CRA)

I help you to pick any two of these three. I suggest however, that the third option usually takes an eternity to get their act together, and to my knowledge, they never ever send a thank-you card. (They are rather self-absorbed like that.)

I work with many doctors. Not one has ever chosen to give financial gifts to the CRA.

Remember. Insurance isn't like winning the lottery.

Not for you, anyway. Because you're dead.

You see, insurance isn't about creating some windfall for your children. You worked hard to get where you are, and you want to ensure your children share your work ethic. I get it.

Nor is life insurance about creating your legacy, or at least not yet.

Insurance is about providing for those who depend on you.

Here's how I like my clients to see how insurance fits in to achieving their goals.

Your financial plan is the engine you build to take you and your family where you want to go, and see what you want to see along the way.

Your income is your engine's fuel, and your insurance is protecting your fuel line.

Without fuel, your engine's not going anywhere. So, you've got to protect your fuel line.

How should you determine what amount of life insurance you need?

If there's one thing I hate about how insurance is often sold, it's HOW it's sold.

First thing. Avoid the sales pitches. You've heard them: they promise you tax-free this or infinite banking that. They're cookie-cutter marketing pitches given to everyone to solve a problem you likely don't even have, rather than a recommendation specific to YOUR needs.

Insurance is also often presented as a race to the bottom to show you the cheapest premiums, *as if that's the only reason anyone would decide to buy it or not.*

"You're the third car salesman in a row that has recommended one of these for us."

The fallacy of the 20x rule

You may have heard advisors say you need 20x your income to be properly protected. The thought behind this is if your life insurance proceeds are invested and get a 5% (1/20th ...) yearly rate of return, the insurance will replace your income stream for your dependents.

Bad idea.

Because you would have bought double your actual life insurance needs.

This is another case of why I don't like how insurance is sold in Canada.

If you're like many of my clients when I first meet with them, you may have:

1. A $700,000 mortgage, a $250,000 student loan, and a $50,000 car loan—all-in your payments are around $7,500 per month

2. Your current lifestyle costs about $10,000 per month

3. You have a savings plan for $2,500 per month

4. You earn $400,000 per year

If we used the outdated 20x rule of thumb to calculate insurance, you'd walk away with an $8,000,000 life insurance policy.

If the proceeds produced 5% every year, the $8,000,000 would never be touched by your dependents.

But that's not why you bought life insurance.

Let me ask you a question though: what is your life insurance designed to replace, your income or what you need to do with it?

When it comes to your insurance, you don't need to set a plate at the dinner table to feed the CRA. Your spending needs are with after-tax dollars, so your insurance needs shouldn't be based on your pre-tax income.

With a need for $20,000 per month (and yes, that's a pretty common occurrence!) of after-tax income, here's how I would calculate your need:

Step 1: Your yearly after tax needs = $240,000

Step 2: For how many years = 20 years

Step 3: How much of your insurance you want left over = $0

Step 4: What rate of return you think the insurance proceeds would receive, less inflation = 5% -3% = 2%

Whipping out my trusty financial calculator, I'd come to $3,924,344 ... or roughly *half the amount of the 20x rule.* Now, maybe $8,000,000 IS what you want. But I like to start with what you NEED, and you can add to that amount if you WANT to do so.

Here's what I recommend to my clients:

We start with knowing your after-tax needed income for planned debt, savings and lifestyle goals (we can plan this!) We then use a rate of return that factors inflation and some tax, and how many years you would otherwise have worked to achieve your goals (ideally at least twenty years).

Ideally, we add any current debt or debt you're thinking of taking on like a mortgage to this number.

I like this approach as it eliminates the concern about your insurance proceeds needing to generate income to pay off debt. Better yet, in my example above, your family would be debt free and only needing to draw $10,000 per month for living expenses. This would allow them to reduce their needed rate of return from 5% to about 3.7% per year.

Once you know the amount of life insurance you NEED, you can decide if you want to go up from there for other goals, or simply set your estate with a guaranteed amount.

It's entirely up to you!

The next step is to get the right TYPE of life insurance.

There are generally two types of life insurance: temporary and permanent—commonly referred to as term or perm.

It's like the choice of renting or purchasing a home.

Both renting a home and buying one have pros and cons, such as cost, flexibility, or length of ownership.

Value and price are two different things.

Price is an issue in the absence of value, when you have no other way to compare. It's important to compare the premium to what it does for you, rather than be the sole consideration.

You want to find the right home within your price range, that meets your current and future needs. It's not likely you only tell your realtor to find you the cheapest home possible (and it might be a bit scary if you did!).

Term insurance is like renting.

You have a much lower premium than a permanent policy, but you don't have anything to show for it when you no longer need the protection. You're paying to have a roof over your head for a period of time.

There are many types of term insurance, but a term 10 or a term 20 are the most common types of term insurance you're likely to encounter.

What are they?

A term 10 or term 20 just means your premiums are guaranteed to not increase for the next ten or twenty years. Most term policies are also known as "RnC", or "Renewable and Convertible" as well. Convertibility is a great feature, allowing you to get term coverage now as you build your financial house, and convert to a permanent coverage later regardless of your health.

Renewable.

At the end of your selected ten or twenty years, your policy automatically renews for another ten or twenty years, subject to whatever is the maximum renewal age of the insurance provider. This means even if your health has changed, they can't take away your coverage on renewal.

That comes with a hefty price-tag however, and you'll likely have sticker shock at the increase. This is because the insurance company is taking the risk on renewal that your health HAS changed, and so they factor in this risk, as well as your older age, into your premiums. It's quite common to see renewals increase premiums by as much as eightfold!

Meet Mark. He Didn't Know Which Insurance to Buy.

Mark, another one of my doctor clients, came to me asking about a mortgage life insurance quote he'd been given. He wanted to see if I could get him cheaper coverage. The quote he'd received was $500,000 to cover most of the amount of his mortgage.

It only took a moment for me to see a major issue.

Mark had been provided a $500,000 life insurance quote for his mortgage, but as a term-10. Why was this an issue?

As a 34-year-old male non-smoker, his annual premiums were about $1,575, which seemed relatively inexpensive. But if we hadn't taken a closer look, it would have become much more costly down the road.

This is because his term-10 policy would renew automatically for a much higher rate for the next ten years, in year 11. In Mark's situation, his policy would have almost doubled to just over $3,300 per year. This means that over twenty years while he had his mortgage, his total premiums paid would be $48,750.

Had he been provided a quote for a policy that wouldn't change for twenty years (a 'term-20'), Mark would save over $5,000 in premiums for the same $500,000 of coverage.

This is another reason I hate the way policies are sold, as they are positioned as the cheapest way to do something, rather than being matched to what you need.

Insurance isn't a commodity. It's an essential component of your sound financial foundation. You don't need cracks in your foundation.

When you go out to find a safe and reliable car to drive your family around, do you tell the car salesman your highest priority is the cheapest car they can find? Or do you look at the safety ratings, reliability and warranty information first, and then find the cheapest car that first fits your needs?

You wouldn't buy a car to protect your family this way. You shouldn't buy insurance to protect you and your family this way either.

Use term life insurance for things you want to protect over your working years such as:

1. Paying off debts

2. Protecting your income

3. Childcare and educational costs

4. Providing for your partner's ability to retire

Permanent policies

Permanent policies on the other hand, are like buying your home with a mortgage. You eventually own your home (just like your insurance, assuming you do your part and pay the premiums of course!), and your base premiums never increase. Since you've gone from a possibility of a claim to a certainty of one however, your premiums are higher than a term policy.

Permanent insurance also allows you to grow some of your wealth sheltered from tax by making additional deposits within it. Given how heavily high-income earners are taxed in Canada, this can be a huge advantage for you as a part of your overall investment strategy *but only when the time is right.*

Notice I never say permanent insurance is more expensive? That's because I like to find the best VALUE for your money, and that depends on what you want to do with it.

There are many ways to use permanent life insurance, from creating a guaranteed tax-free estate to building wealth sheltered from tax or even using it to help create a tax-efficient retirement income stream, but always remember this:

The best life insurance is the one that's in force at the time you pass away.

There's no right or wrong answer here.

Term insurance allows you to put most of your money toward other things that are important to you, such as eliminating your debt or growing your savings. Permanent insurance is there when needed, won't increase in price, and it keeps the taxman away from what you've worked hard to earn.

What matters to YOU is what's important.

———•———

Chapter Summary Lessons:

1. Start with term, you can always convert later when you're more established.

2. Get the term that covers your need, not just the one that's cheap (it will likely become your most expensive).

3. Cheapest doesn't equate to best. Don't pick based on the cheapest quote, but the one that suits your needs instead.

CHAPTER 9

When To Buy Permanent Insurance

MY ACCOUNTANT ONCE ASKED ME HOW I determine how much permanent insurance to recommend for a client. I think my answer surprised him.

"Nobody I've ever met has come to me saying they want to have enough permanent life insurance for their "funeral and final expenses", yet I see those kinds of policies being sold all the time."

I told him there are so many factors to consider, that I don't believe there are any set calculations you can use.

Let me explain why.

It Happened. You Were Hit By A Bus.

I can calculate with a fair degree of accuracy what your estate liability would be like if you walked out of my office and got hit by that maniac bus driver everyone keeps talking about.

But there's more to it.

When you look out further, there are several complicating factors such as:

1. **How are your assets taxed?** Your home is tax-free but your RSP can be fully taxable.

2. **Will your assets grow**, stay the same, or be depleted through retirement?

3. **What liabilities** might you have left in the future?

4. **What are future tax rates** going to be? (Psssssst ... they won't be lower.)

Recently my parents sold their vacation property at Whistler, B.C. Honestly, while I couldn't help but be a little sad it was gone after so many years, I was also relieved.

I have a brother in Vancouver and a sister in Sweden. Had my parents not sold their property, eventually my siblings and I would have to determine what to do with it. My brother could use it more often than any of us, while my sister would rarely use it and me somewhere in-between. By selling it, our parents have relieved us of a potential conflict in dealing with their estate.

But what if our parents had wanted to keep their property?

Insurance can help there as well in equalizing their estate. Maybe my brother would want to keep the property, and instead we receive other assets. Or they could have insurance in place so my sister and I receive the equivalent value of the property my brother might inherit. Insurance can even be in place to pay for the anticipated tax as their property transfers to him.

My point here is that everyone's permanent needs are different, and there really can't be a one-size-fits-all solution.

So, here's my answer that surprised my accountant.

You don't get permanent insurance.

At least not until you have a specific need.

Instead, I recommend my clients get the term amount for their hit-by-that-maniac-bus-driver today liability, so at least we have that covered. We can convert later to a permanent policy (remember I said they were renewable AND convertible?) when the need arises and it's strategic to do so.

There's no cost to convert and being able to do so is a feature in your term policy. While you'll be a bit older when we may decide to change it, we can also spend more time figuring out what amount is appropriate for your estate, or even how we can use it to create tax-free retirement income.

Here's when to use permanent insurance:

1. When you have a known future tax liability, such as with an estate freeze or to keep a vacation property within the family.

2. When you want to equalize your estate. That same vacation property might be great for one of your children, but not practical for another to use. Permanent insurance can replace the value of what you give to one child.

3. You want to supercharge a gift to your charity.

4. When you have wealth, you want to protect from market volatility, and create tax-efficient retirement income or transfer your excess corporate savings to your children.

And when you head home today?

Stay away from the buses.

Chapter Summary Lessons:

1. Have a permanent insurance for a permanent need.

2. Equal doesn't mean fair for your estate—insurance can help equalize.

3. There is no cookie-cutter approach that can be used for your timing or need for permanent insurance.

CHAPTER 10

Critical Illness Insurance

CRITICAL ILLNESS INSURANCE IS DESIGNED TO protect you from the financial impact of a life-threatening illness such as cancer, stroke or a heart attack. It may surprise you to know however, how this protection was created.

It wasn't designed by some actuary sitting in the 18th floor of an insurance company. It was actually Dr. Marius Barnard, a South African cardiac surgeon, who saw the urgent need for this protection for his patients.

If that name sounds familiar to you, it may be because he was on the team, headed by his brother Dr. Christiaan Barnard, who performed the world's first human to human heart transplant in 1967.

Dr. Barnard had a patient who was a 34-year-old single mother who was in the last stages of terminal lung cancer. When he asked her why she hadn't come to see him earlier, she replied that she had to work. Dr. Barnard was struck with the realization that his patients not only had physical crises, but financial ones as well when faced with a critical illness. Over the coming years, he worked with insurance companies to develop this gap in protection.

Sadly, Dr. Barnard passed away in 2014, but not before creating a video on why he felt so strongly this coverage was needed for his patients.

Go Take A Look!

THIS SHORT BUT POWERFUL video explains why he pushed so hard to correct the gap in people's protection.

Meet Samantha. My First Insurance Claim.

I can relate to Dr. Barnard's experience, at least from the perspective of my very first insurance claim I processed on behalf of one of my clients.

Samantha was also a single mother in her early 30s, and just three months after we put her protection in place, she came to me for advice. Her oncologist had told her she had cancer.

She was still alive, so there was no life insurance payout. She was also still able to work while she went through treatment, so she was unable to collect on her company's disability policy.

But fortunately, she DID have the right coverage with her critical illness, and two weeks after I submitted her claim, she had a cheque in hand to cover all of her family's expenses for the next couple of years.

It was one of the proudest yet humbling experiences of my life to be able to deliver on a promise for someone when they're at their lowest point.

I'm happy to tell you that she's still with us today.

———•———

When "Free" isn't a good idea for your critical illness protection.

Meet Jessica. When Free Isn't Free.

Jessica, a new client, recently brought in her policies for me to review.

As I pored over her paperwork, I noticed she had a $150,000 critical illness policy with a return of premiums in fifteen years. She'd been told if she didn't ever have a claim, her premiums would be returned upon surrendering her policy at year 15 for about $60,000, making it a 'free' policy.

She was also shown her risks. For her age and non-smoking status, one insurer estimated Jessica's odds of having a disability (28%), critical illness (19%), or prematurely passing away (5%.)

I was so frustrated! Not with her of course, but with Mr. Salesman who sold her that policy.

Okay, I'll explain why I was so ticked off.

Critical illness is designed to provide a lump-sum of cash in the event of an illness such as cancer, heart attack and stroke. While many policies cover a wide range of potential other illnesses, these three often account for 85-90% of all claims received by an insurer. But with today's medical advances, you have a much higher chance of surviving physically. The financial impact however, can do long-lasting damage to achieving your goals.

After a major health event, you may not even WANT to work as hard as you have been. The odds are high that you'd want to focus more on enjoying life and family, which itself, is a financial impact to you.

This is the reason you should get your protection in place. I know—a "Free Policy" looks like you get the best of both worlds. Full protection AND all your money back.

Sounds good, but not for Jessica's situation.

A "Free Policy" isn't that simple, and it also

doesn't reflect what really happens.

Jessica wasn't shown how, for the same premiums she was paying for the $150,000 "Free Policy", she could have over $600,000 of term coverage for the next twenty years (albeit she wouldn't have her premiums refunded). That's 4x the coverage!

Here's the show-stopper. Jessica should have been shown two options:

Option 1: The "free" coverage. $150,000 of protection during the next fifteen years. All of her premiums returned, but with an effective loss (I would call the actual cost) due to inflation of $26,500.

Option 2: The 'not-free' coverage. $600,000 of protection during the next fifteen years. While no premiums are returned, her effective cost after inflation would be $25,325.

That's right.

Because of the higher premiums she'd need to pay to get all of her premiums back if she didn't have a claim, she was effectively paying MORE for only a quarter of the protection she could have obtained with a term policy where she didn't get her premiums back.

And that more expensive/lower protection option would only return her premiums if she didn't have a claim. And if she did have a claim, it would mean she had significantly overpaid for only

$150,000 worth of coverage, since she had paid for her premiums to be refunded which now wouldn't happen. I'm guessing she'd much rather have $600,000 coming to her instead.

Yeah. My blood is boiling again.

And here's something else to wrap your head around.

A critical illness policy IS NOT A SAVINGS ACCOUNT.

You might wonder what is the purpose of insurance—is it a forced savings plan, or is it your financial lifeline when you need it?

A critical illness policy is always meant to be a financial lifeline when you need it.

This brings me back to those misleading statistics Jessica was shown by Mr. Salesman.

I went to the insurer's online calculator he'd used and noticed something—see if you can spot it.

I re-ran her odds if she was a smoker, and the calculator came back saying her risk of a disability was 28%, with her risk of a critical illness at 19%, and prematurely passing away at 13%. Her combined risk of one of these three happening to her was now 45%. According to this calculator, one in every two female smokers her age would be impacted, apparently.

Did you catch what I noticed?

Only one number had changed—her odds of prematurely passing away.

Wait a second.

But Jessica was a non-smoker! And her policy and investment should reflect that.

This calculator from a major insurance company showed there was no increased risk for a critical illness such as cancer, heart attack or stroke if she was a smoker.

White papers from around the world show how detrimental smoking is to your health. I'm not a doctor, but even I felt this wasn't medically right.

When I dug deeper into their data, I found out why. They were getting their statistics from sources that, while reputable and well known, *don't distinguish occurrences between smoker and non-smoker*, only by age and gender.

Instead, the statistics Mr. Salesman had shown her had over-estimated her odds of having a health event as a non-smoker. Yes, she needed to protect her income. But neither should her risks have been overestimated.

Yet another case of numbers that aren't lying, but they are still misleading. I notified the insurance company about this issue, but when I last checked, nothing had changed.

So frustrating.

Fortunately, Jessica and I met early on in her career, and we developed a plan that made sense for her.

Building your insurance portfolio is a lot like building your house. You don't go and buy the furniture first, and then design your house around it. You build the blueprints for the house you want, and then find the furniture that fits your design.

You Need Critical Illness Insurance. It Just Has To Be The Right Fit.

The odds you'll experience a health event are still significant enough that I strongly recommend you consider some critical illness protection.

Remember, it's not just you who might have income reduced, but your partner as well. They may need to help with your care, they may have to quit their job or reduce their hours, and they'll definitely take on more of the household and family needs.

It's not a piece of cake for anyone involved. And the stress is through the roof.

Generally, I'm a fan of term critical illness coverage over permanent. I want you to have the amount of coverage you need while you're working, instead of leaving you exposed with less protection in order to afford a policy that is 'free'.

———•———

There are mercifully fewer features on most critical illness policies, and while some have stand-alone benefits, I'll help you wade through the two common ones.

A) Return of premium on death. (ROPD)

Simply put, should you die while your policy is in place, all your premiums are returned to the policy owner, most likely your estate.

This is a commonly sold benefit since it's a fairly inexpensive option to not 'lose' your money if you die. *Don't buy it if you can obtain term life insurance.*

Why? There are three reasons life insurance is a better option.

1. Even though ROPD riders are inexpensive, you can most likely get more coverage on a term life policy for the same premiums.

2. You can get rid of the critical illness policy when you've saved enough to not worry about the financial impact of a serious illness, without reducing what will be paid

out on your death by having that amount on your life insurance instead.

3.   If you're incorporated into a Professional Corporation, an RoPD just gives your money back, but it's still trapped in your company—there's taxes to be paid to get it out to your estate. Life insurance however, has the benefit of being able to be paid out tax-free.

More coverage, better taxation, and you can keep your coverage when you no longer need your critical illness protection.

B) Return of premium on expiry, or surrender or expiry. (ROPX/S)

Unlike disability, if you hold your critical illness policy for the required fifteen or twenty years, you get ALL of your premiums back, not just half. Of course, if you had a claim, you probably won't have a policy anymore as it would likely have been paid out to you and ended.

Now you may like the thought of not 'wasting' your premiums. Many of my clients feel the same way.

Let's have a look at Mark's situation.

My client Mark hated the thought of his premiums just going *POOF* every year. He knew he needed coverage though, and was provided a quote for $500,000 with annual premiums of almost $5,500 per year for forty years to age 65. He'd pay a whopping $220,000 over those forty years for coverage that he likely wouldn't need past age 50 anyway, assuming he had properly saved for retirement.

RoPX/S riders aren't available on most term 10 or 20 policies, but instead require you to have a term to 65, 75 or 100 (these are called permanent policies for critical illness).

Because Mark hated the thought of losing money on his premiums paid, he wanted to have his premiums refunded. But that meant he needed a policy that he'd be paying for long after he had the ability to retire.

But the fun didn't stop there, since the term to 65 was just the base. He also had to have the RoPX/S rider added, which brought his premiums to just over $10,000 per year. Yowza.

We found a much better option for Mark.

A term-20 policy for the same coverage was only $3,160 per year. With the remaining $7,000 difference, we put that toward his mortgage. That saved Mark $136,000 in interest and knocked seven years off his mortgage. A much better solution!

This is why it's so important to have the right coverage plan that fits your life plans.

Listen, I get the appeal of what can seem like free coverage, or not wanting to feel like your premiums are 'wasted'. But you need to crunch the numbers, or have me do it for you.

One last thing.

Premiums aren't a waste.

You're buying something each month that acts as an invisible protective shield around you and your family.

You're not just buying "air."

A Lesson From My Childhood Best Friend

My childhood best friend, Matthew, bought only a $50,000 critical illness policy several years ago from his insurance advisor. He was in his early 30s with a young family, a new mortgage, and years of earning power ahead of him. While his financial risks were high, he didn't think he'd ever need his coverage.

As fate would have it, it was only a few years later when he developed prostate cancer. I'm so thankful to our medical system that he's alive and kicking today; and he's a believer and thankful for his policy. That $50,000 allowed him to know their bills would be paid for the next couple of years so he could just focus on his health.

I'm also thankful he was able to return to work full-time. He's one of the lucky ones who has made a full recovery.

But there's a problem.

Even though he's now a believer in how important it is for him to have coverage should cancer return, or he has some other major health event—he can't buy another critical illness policy for at least five years, and when he can, it will most likely be rated (he'll have to pay a higher premium to offset the increased risk of a second event happening.)

Things could have been easier for Matthew.

If he'd been provided a proper plan first, which had recommended the proper amount of coverage he needed, balanced against his other goals for his income—the financial stress levels—then and now, would've been dramatically less.

How would his experience have changed if he'd enough coverage to ensure at least two years of their needed income, giving him enough time to recover without financial stress?

You buy insurance to protect you and your family against the financial impact of a health event, not to make some salesperson's quota.

What Kind Of Critical Insurance Should You Buy?

Let's start with the two basics.

1. How much coverage do you need?

At a minimum, I like to see enough to cover your debts plus two years of your needed after-tax income.

This allows you to not stress about debt, while also giving you a two-year window to help you partially or fully recover. If partially, then you have time to adjust your finances.

Some of my clients choose to go for higher coverage than this, to help protect their ability to save, as well as for other reasons.

2. How long do you need critical illness coverage?

The other thing you need to determine is for how long you need your coverage.

I know. You have no idea! Don't worry about it—my clients don't know at first either!

My short answer is this: if you could retire today, you no longer need your coverage.

Until that time, protect your a$$ets and your income.

A Critical Illness Formula I Recommend To My Clients:

How much coverage should you purchase?

In addition to two years of needed income (and ideally any debt you don't want to have to worry about while you're recovering!), there's another question.

How long should your critical insurance coverage extend to?

I tell my clients to get two policies to match your length of term with your length of need.

Consider a term-10 for car loans, student loans, credit card balances—generally things with ten years or less remaining to be paid out, then drop the policy.

Consider a term-20 for longer needs such as your mortgage, or while your children are young.

You'll save hundreds, if not thousands of dollars, with a cheaper policy for your shorter needs, by not increasing your coverage for your longer-term needs.

Remember. The planning here should always be unique to you.

Don't let anyone tell you differently.

Should you purchase critical illness policies for your kids?

And here's a tough question I get asked a lot.

"Should I have critical illness on my children?"

For many years, I had the honour of being the coach and steersperson for the Children's Wish Dragonboat team. Our goal was to raise at least $10,000 per year, which was the average cost of a wish for a child with a life-threatening illness.

As a side moment of pride in our team, in ten years we raised over $500,000 for some of the most amazing children you could hope to meet. I can't write this even now without my eyes tearing up, thinking of these kids we met who were simply amazing in every way.

It was heartbreaking, however, to see the financial impact the children's illnesses had on their families. Their parents were often torn between having to work, spend money on travel, accommodation, food, fuel, medications, special treatments and sometimes juggling childcare for siblings too.

I'm sure you've met families like this in your practice.

They just want to spend every moment by their child's side.

But I've often seen this gap in families' coverage.

Now I'll be the first to admit the odds of children having a life-threatening illness like cancer are low, however, I've seen first-hand the impact for those unlucky families whose children we were trying to grant wishes for.

More than that, I also have a very personal reason for recommending my clients at least consider proper coverage for their children.

My wife's friend Memory and her husband had just welcomed their first child. About a month or so after their daughter's delivery, Memory was admitted to the hospital for some health issues arising from childbirth. They discovered it was from cancer.

Memory spent the next year in the Tom Baker Cancer Centre, and despite having a 5-year survival rate of over 90%, she died.

A few years later, cancer returned to their household. Her young daughter had developed cancer. What followed next were several years of highs and lows, but eventually her daughter also passed away.

I can't imagine the pain Memory's husband went through. He was with his wife and daughter through everything and never left their sides. I don't know what the impact was financially, but I was determined to ensure my wife and I would never have to find out for ourselves.

My wife and I have critical illness protection in place on each of our children.

You see, this isn't about protecting income (as our children don't earn income.)

This is insurance we never want to collect on. But if something should ever happen, the policies would provide funds to ensure we can be exactly where we want to be, with our kids, and not have to worry about our jobs and paying the bills.

Even better, with the policies I obtained for them—they're paid up now. And when my kids turn 25, if they haven't had a claim, three quarters of all premiums I've paid are returned to them AND their policies stay in force for life.

My wife and I can be with our children if something ever happens, and when they become adults, it helps protect their income for life, too.

I hope they never have to use them.

I hope no one ever does.

———•———

Chapter Summary Lessons:

1. When a family member has a serious illness, everyone's income is affected.

2. Term coverage for what you need, you've got better options for the rest of your money.

3. Protecting your children protects you as well.

CHAPTER 11

Why You Need Disability Insurance

I WAS OUT FOR DINNER WITH a friend of mine, who also happens to be a doctor. Lucas had just passed his last exams and was interested to know what he should do to start off on the right financial path.

What I really enjoyed about the evening was an agreement we made before we got together—my condition for helping him was that he couldn't buy anything from me.

To remove any chance of bias in my recommendations to a friend, my 'fee' that night was his turn to pick up the tab for the mountain of chicken wings we were devouring.

That may sound odd, since my business is helping doctors in all areas of their financial life. But my competition isn't another advisor. What I'm driven by is helping doctors be secure before one of two things happens:

1. You have a health event that causes financial hardship to you and those you care about.

2. To get you proper and unbiased information before you meet a salesperson who sees you as a dollar sign.

Lucas waved a chicken wing in the air.

"An insurance guy came to the hospital today, and showed our team why we should get his disability protection." Lucas said. "What do you think?"

I knew how hard Lucas had worked to get where he was. I also knew how hard doctors work and often without any financial safety net except those they purchase themselves.

"Absolutely—you'd be crazy not to. What did the guy say you should do?" I asked.

Lucas slid a package across the table that everyone had been provided. It was a proposal for $3,500 per month of coverage, with all the bells and whistles.

I inwardly winced at what I saw, and said, "Let's order another round of drinks, we're going to be a while."

What had I seen in the disability proposal that made me sigh? Several things.

First, what's with the $3,500 per month coverage?

I'll tell you why.

It's because $3,500/month is typically what disability insurance carriers will allow without financially qualifying. In order to get insurance, you often not only have to qualify with your health, but also your income. So, for students this can be a great start. For a resident like Lucas however, it was already lower than they could get approved for and I suspect this was being offered as an 'easy' sale rather than helping him based on his income and needs.

There was a *Future Income Option* (FIO), sometimes also called a *Guaranteed Income Option*, which would allow him to add on an additional $12,000 later. I do like FIOs when you anticipate earning more in the future, as they allow you to obtain more coverage regardless of a change in health, as long as you financially qualify for more.

But as Lucas's FIO only allowed him to increase his protection by $3,000 per year, it would take him four years to maximize his $12,000. Meanwhile, he'd be significantly underinsured. And each yearly increase would be based on his age *then* instead of *now*.

His proposal also had a *Return of Premium* (RoP) rider. It makes for a great sales pitch. If you go eight years without a claim, you get half your money back. What's not to love?

Plenty as it turns out. Let me show you what I mean.

Let's assume the annual premium for your disability is $2,000 per year. Since most RoP riders are about half the cost of the base premium, we'll add an extra $1,000 per year for a total annual premium of $3,000.

Assuming you didn't get rid of your policy, after eight years one of two things would be true: either you've had a disability, or you haven't.

If you had a disability, then in hindsight you've overpaid for your protection as you could have paid $2,000 per year, but instead paid $3,000 per year and now you won't receive a refund. No way to know this except in the rear-view mirror, however.

But what if you didn't have a disability? You can now look forward to a cheque for half of your premiums, right? Well … sort of.

Had you gone without the RoP, then over the eight years you'd have paid $16,000. Instead, you paid $24,000, received $12,000 back, and had a net cost of $12,000 paid. That's a 25% reduction from the $16,000 you could have paid, not 'half back' as is usually marketed.

You with me?

Taking it a step further, what if you had instead saved that extra $1,000 within your company (disability policies are almost always owned personally—I'll cover why in a later chapter) and received just a 3% return per year? In eight years, you'd have paid only $16,000, but would also have about $10,000 in savings.

In the first option with return of premium, you're out $12,000 ($24,000 paid, half back.) In the option where you saved the RoP amount instead, you're a net "out" of $6,000 ($16,000 paid, $10,000 saved). In other words, saving your money instead is both the cheaper option, and would happen without the gamble of whether you'll have a disability.

I don't mind if you choose to get this rider. What I object to is how it's sold by people who either haven't done the math, or have done the math, but hope you won't.

Check Into Your Medical Association Disability Plans

"Lucas, have you taken a look at what your medical association offers for disability?" I asked. "It's considerably cheaper, and while your premiums do increase with age, it's often not until your 50s before they're even close in cost. By then, you'd likely not even need your disability protection anyway. They're similar in coverages, and you could probably get more coverage out of the gate at a lower cost to boot."

Lucas hadn't thought of that as he's new to the game. But your medical association is an excellent place to get affordable disability insurance.

Group plans are usually a good deal less expensive since your association has large negotiation power with so many doctors, but also for the insurance carrier the risk is spread over a larger number of doctors not just you.

I connected Lucas with his AMA representative, and we continued with our chicken wings and beer evening.

Later as we got up to leave, we were interrupted by a friend of his—another doctor who was in the booth beside us. I assumed he just wanted to say hi to Lucas, but he turned to me and asked for my business card. Turns out, he'd heard me advising my friend to go to his association for his disability insurance, and liked that advice was being given that was best for Lucas and not a commission for me!

I've always believed if you do what's right for the person who's entrusting you with their financial future—it all comes back to you. It's fundamental in building long-term trust, and his friend who was eavesdropping? He's now one of my favourite clients as we share a similar mindset.

———•———

I'm not going to go on at length about why you need disability protection. You've taken years to get here, taken a lot of risk, and sacrificed a ton.

Protecting what you've accomplished with disability insurance isn't a question—just do it.

But what do I like to see for disability insurance, regardless of where you get it from?

1. **I want you to get the maximum amount of coverage now, up to the amount you need for your financial plan to stay on track if you should have a disability.** You don't want to be run the risk of a disability leaving you with a gap if it should happen before you've been able to get all of your Future Income Option room. You'll pay a lower rate getting full coverage today as well, BUT you need to have a proper financial plan first, not a sales pitch about getting half back. Insurance is for guarantees, not gambling.

2. **Have an elimination period of 90 days.** Think of this like a deductible on your car insurance—the longer the elimination period (higher the deductible) before you can receive benefits, the lower your premiums. At 30 days your premiums are basically about double versus 90 days, but going the other way at 180 days—it's only around 5% less. Ninety days is your sweet spot.

3. **Ensure your policy covers you to age 65.** I've seen too many people only with coverage periods of two or five years in order to reduce their premiums. My opinion? If you're disabled for two or five years, it's likely you have a permanent disability. Going with two or five years is a gamble on how long you would be disabled, rather than protecting yourself FROM being disabled. Get coverage

to age 65 every time—you can always drop it earlier when you no longer need it.

4. **Have an Own Occupation definition.** Disability has three definitions: any, regular and own occupation. I've had many surgeons (for example) who told me that if they can't be in the OR, they don't want to teach or do anything else. Since considering Any or Regular is gambling with coverage when you need it in order to have a 'cheaper' premium? I'm going to save you time and frustration here.

Own Occupation … all the way.

If you're planning on staying a doctor—and I suspect you are—get disability insurance from your medical association, and ensure you have the riders I mentioned. There are nuances where having your own policy can make sense, but start with your association so you're covered, then see if your financial plan says otherwise.

And this is the same conversation I had with Lucas over chicken wings and beer.

Aren't you glad you're here to eavesdrop?

———•———

Disability vs Critical Illness. It's An Apple and Orange Situation.

Apples and oranges are both fruits but they aren't the same.

My clients initially often feel there's an overlap or duplication with disability and critical illness. While I understand this confusion, there are two big differences.

The first difference comes from what kind of health issue has been claimed.

Disability and Critical illness have one thing in common—you've had/have a health issue.

And that's where the similarity ends.

For most disability policies, the largest number of claims usually arise from musculoskeletal, depression and anxiety (collectively taking up to a third of claims.) Surprisingly, cancer often comes in fifth, at less than 10% of disability claims.

Compare that to critical illness where the lion's share of claims is from cancer. Usually around two thirds of all claims. In fact, cancer, heart attacks and strokes are typically around 85% of claims. (Contrary to popular belief of these illnesses affecting older Canadians, the majority of these claims are from Canadians in their prime working years.)

Disability payments are also received monthly, and can start/stop/re-start as you go on or off claim. (I'll go into greater detail in the next chapter.)

With a critical illness policy, it's one and done in most cases.

Your coverage is paid to you as a lump-sum and tax-free. While some policies have a "second event" rider, in most cases your policy would be done, leaving you without coverage. Once you've had a claim, getting a new policy later is much harder to obtain. This is exactly what happened to my best friend.

I'd want you to have the maximum disability coverage you can obtain, since it's the most likely to happen to you.

Follow that up with at least 2 years of your after-tax needed amount of critical illness.

You'll be in a good position to avoid having to make rash financial decisions should your health take a turn for the worse.

———•———

Chapter Summary Lessons:

1. Disability is the most likely to happen, but unless you're changing careers your association's coverage will likely fit the bill.

2. Disability is NOT the same as Critical Illness—you need both. Maximize your disability and have at least two years' needed income for your Critical Illness.

3. If you're recommended return of premium on your disability? Don't walk ... run!

CHAPTER 12

How To Hold Your Policies

WHEN I WORK WITH A DOCTOR to get their proper risk management portfolio in place, two questions always come up:

1. **Can I deduct the premiums?**

2. **Can I own the policy in my company?**

Remember. Disability insurance, critical illness and life insurance are three different cats.

For the majority of my clients, here's what I recommend:

Disability

Taxes: Should you deduct the premiums? Nope.

Deducting premiums is like winning the battle, but losing the war. It can feel great to make your premiums feel cheaper, but you could end up paying far more in taxes. Let me explain.

If you pay your disability premiums with after-tax dollars, the CRA allows you to receive any benefit when you're disabled also as tax-free.

The reverse is also true. If you have a pre-tax premium (i.e. you deducted your premiums from your income tax), you'll have a pre-tax benefit.

Source: Canada.ca: Disability insurance benefits and taxes

"Generally, if you pay the entire amount of the disability premium yourself, your disability benefits will be tax-free. This may bring your income while on disability closer to your current take-home pay.

If your employer pays all or part of the disability premium, your disability benefits will be subject to income taxes."

You're your own employer. If you deduct your premiums, you'll pay income tax on your benefits when you're already experiencing a big income reduction from being disabled.

Don't do it.

Who Owns The Policy?

If you've purchased your disability protection from your Medical Association's group plan, the question of how it's owned is answered for you. You don't own it, your Association does.

You are the insured, payor, and beneficiary of the policy however, and should you have a qualified claim you'd receive your monthly benefit personally since you've paid for the premiums with after-tax personal dollars.

If you own your own policy, you can own it in your company, but I don't suggest it. If you owned your policy within your Professional Corporation, your premiums would come into your company tax-free, but you'd have to pay personal income-tax to get it out to your jeans.

IF YOU HOLD SOME of your debt within your company such as a mortgage on a rental property, you may want to have two policies (personal for personal debt, corporate for corporate debt.) You could save hundreds per year this way, since your disability in your company isn't needed to pay out to you personally—you'd use it to make your corporate debt payments. In this case, the tax savings on your premium would like far exceed a second policy fee.

For most doctors, just own your policy personally and don't deduct the premiums.

Critical Illness

Taxes: Should you deduct the premiums? Also, nope.

The same reasons not to deduct your critical illness premiums for disability also apply for critical illness—even more. You generally can't deduct your critical illness premiums anyway, but there's a big reason you wouldn't want to even if you could.

Remember, a critical illness payment arrives as a lump sum.

Because it arrives as a lump sum, you DEFINITELY wouldn't want to have it be taxable. Our progressive tax system takes an even larger bite of your taxable income the more you are considered to have earned in a year. And that critical illness payment would likely take you into a higher tax bracket and could have you giving half your benefit to the government!

Again, don't deduct it.

Who Should Own The Critical Illness Policy?

Where to hold your policy however, does differ from disability.

In the event you were to suffer a serious illness and have a qualified claim paid to you, you're not likely to be able to pay out all of your debt at once due to huge pre-payment penalties on mortgages anyway. It might make sense then, to hold your policy in your company and pay yourself dividends in the amount and frequency you would have paid yourself normally.

And if you don't have a health event and eventually get rid of your policy, you've saved thousands in taxes compared to having owned the policy personally since you got to pay your premiums with lightly taxed corporate dollars rather than paying with much higher-taxed personal dollars.

If, however, the thought of having debt while facing a significant life event really bothers you? Then I strongly advocate for holding your policy personally. Should you have a valid claim, your policy will be received tax-free and you can just focus on your health and not your mortgage.

There isn't a right or wrong answer here. It depends on both your values as well as where you hold your debt and other expenses. Proper planning helps you know the difference!

Life Insurance

Taxes: Should you deduct the premiums? It depends!

Now life insurance is a whole other beast.

While it still is often best not to deduct your premiums, the most common exception to this is when the life insurance is a requirement for a business loan.

Maybe you're looking to buy into a separate business or to start up your own, and the bank requires you to provide a copy of your life insurance, as well as assigning it to them to cover your loan should you prematurely die. In that instance, your insurance premiums may be deductible while still being able to be received without tax.

Watch out for a common mistake I encounter here though.

It's not technically the life insurance premiums that are deductible, but rather what's known as the *"Net Cost of Pure Insurance"* (NCPI) portion of the premiums that's deductible. If your situation is such that you'd be able to deduct your insurance premiums, ensure you get your insurance company to provide your accountant with a NCPI table, which tells the accountant how much they can deduct each year.

This mix-up isn't that big a deal if you have term insurance, but I've often seen the larger premiums of a permanent insurance being fully deducted.

A big no-no, as you'd be deducting far more than what's allowable.

Let's keep the CRA off your back!

Who Owns The Life Insurance Policy?

Unlike disability, life insurance is almost always held in your company.

If you outlive your need for term insurance and eventually surrender or let your policy lapse, you only ever paid lightly taxed corporation premiums.

If you were to prematurely die however, life insurance is treated favourably within a company:

1. The death benefit is received tax-free to your company.

2. The death benefit (excluding any cash values) doesn't add to the value of your shares when they're assessed for tax in your terminal return.

3. The death benefit less the *Adjusted Cost Basis* of the policy can be paid out tax-free to your estate. And your accountant can rest easy here—insurance companies usually provide this information with the claim payout.

In most cases, hold your life insurance within your company and ensure you're deducting the right amount if it's able to be deducted.

You're in the same situation if you die, but if you outlive your coverage? You've saved thousands in taxes on your premiums.

———•———

Chapter Summary Lessons:

1. Hold your policy where it's needed.

2. Two policies can work better than one in the wrong place.

3. Don't win the battle but lose the war. Only deduct your premiums when appropriate.

CHAPTER 13

Creditor Protection Insurance

I USED TO WORK AT SOME of Canada's largest financial institutions, and when I was a loans officer I was trained to say, "Your loan (or mortgage) payments, including life insurance protection, are this much per month."

Ostensibly, this protection when you get your mortgage means your mortgage would be paid off should you die, or your mortgage payments covered while you're disabled. In reality, you're wearing the Emperor's New Clothes—which means you really don't have any protection.

I really didn't like selling protection that way. Worse, there are many reasons I view creditor protection as barely better than no insurance at all.

Creditor protection seems so easy to get. There are typically only four or five questions, no bloodwork or urinalysis, and approval is usually automatic if you answer no to their questions.

All those questions do however, is allow you to start paying premiums. It does NOT mean you're certain to have your protection in place.

My Top 7 Reasons Against Creditor Protection. Just Say No.

1. Creditor life insurance is often limited to $750,000 maximum coverage.

Recently one of my doctors was obtaining a new mortgage for $1.2 million, and was wondering why their mortgage was split into two quotes. It only took a moment to see what had happened. Their bank advisor had one quote for $750,000 with their creditor insurance, and the other quote was for the balance of their mortgage and without any protection on it because their maximum coverage was on the first quote.

2. Limited disability payouts.

Disability coverage is often limited to only 24 months of coverage, to a maximum of $3,000 per month. Guess what? If you're disabled for two years, I bet your disability is likely permanent. But your coverage certainly isn't. And if your mortgage payments are higher than $3,000 per month, you're on the hook for the rest even though you're disabled. I've never heard of this limitation of amount and coverage length being explained to a client.

3. Pre-claim versus post-claim underwriting.

This is a HUGE one. When you get proper insurance, you go through an extensive array of health questions, and often must provide medical evidence (typically bloodwork and urinalysis), as well as a report from your family doctor. If you get covered, you KNOW you're covered.

With creditor protection, the decision on whether your policy will pay out is made AFTER a claim is made and it's too late to make adjustments to your financial plan. You, or your family, may then discover your claim is denied for some health reason and instead of a payout, your premiums are simply refunded. But your mortgage is still owing.

4. Everyone has a hand in your pocket.

In many cases, your premiums are actually higher than if you went out to get your own term life insurance or disability coverage. Why is that? Well, both the bank and their insurance company are taking a slice. When you get your own coverage, the bank's fingers don't get in the pie.

5. If your health changes, you're stuck.

What if another bank has better rates, easier repayment terms, or offers you discounts on other services if you transfer your mortgage? If your health has changed, you may be stuck at your current bank since your creditor protection can't transfer with your mortgage and your new lender isn't likely to offer coverage.

6. You pay a level premium for a decreasing benefit.

As you pay down your mortgage, the amount your creditor protection needs to pay out to cover your mortgage also decreases.

I've met with many doctors who thought they were covered with 'life insurance' from their bank, only to be surprised to learn their coverage was far less than they had thought.

7. The lender decides how a payout is allocated, not you.

For many Canadians, a mortgage is often their cheapest debt when compared to car or student loans, credit cards or lines of credit. Or maybe they could free up cash flow by paying off one or more outstanding debts *instead* of their mortgage, or you may have wanted to fund your children's education or help for your partner's ability to retire. If this is you, bad news. The bank will payout what you owe them instead.

If you ever wondered why it's called 'creditor protection', now you know: it protects the creditor, not you.

If you're presented with this option when you get your loan or mortgage, I would get it temporarily, and then cancel it as soon as you get proper insurance elsewhere.

———•———

Chapter Summary Lessons:

1. Creditor protection protects the creditor, not you.

2. Your family may be surprised to learn you were never actually covered.

3. Your own policy is likely cheaper, and has far more certainty.

Principle Five: Save It

It's time in the markets, not market timing, that's your recipe for success.

Let's get time working for you, shall we?

CHAPTER 14

How Much to Save For Retirement?

I MET ANITA WHEN I WAS giving a talk at the Cumming School of Medicine, and she definitely was prepared. After everyone had left, we sat down in the cafeteria for a coffee, and she flipped open her binder and passed me an investment proposal she'd received from her banker.

"She said if I started now, I could have $5,000,000 by the time I retire."

Anita then asked a question which may seem like it would have an obvious answer, but I've lost track of the number of times I've been asked it.

"Adrian, will five million be enough?"

I looked at her and said,

"It depends!"

It's one thing to know what we can expect to earn and spend.

It's an entirely different beast to know how much you need to have saved, in order to continue to spend that the same amount AND never outlive your savings. You have to consider the impacts from future tax rates, health costs, inflation and market volatility, just to name a few.

I looked at the proposal. On the front page was a net worth statement showing:

Anita's Planned Retirement Age: 55

$520,000 in a Tax-Free Savings Account $1,130,000 in a Retirement Savings Plan $3,310,000 in Corporate Savings

But there was a HUGE PROBLEM.

It wasn't Anita's true net worth.

Most net worth calculators fall victim to this problem.

Her banker had put her *Tax-Free Savings Account* (tax-free money) beside her *RSP* (fully taxable when withdrawn) and bumped them up against her lightly-taxed corporate savings (which would have income taxes payable to withdraw to her personal bank account) and declared her to be worth $5,000,000 at age 55.

Her true net worth after-taxes would be considerably less.

It also was completely irrelevant.

I looked at Anita and asked,

"Why did you choose 55 to stop working?"

Anita answered, "Oh, that's not a number I chose. She just said I could be retired by then."

I took a deep breath, and resisted the urge to show what was wrong with the proposal. Instead, I asked her to forget about retirement for the moment, and to tell me what she hoped the next five years would look like.

Like many younger doctors, she was excited to start her practice, buy a home, pay off her student loans, and enjoy life after being in school for so long. (And finally, being able to eat more than late night Kraft Dinner.)

What wasn't on her priority list? That she wanted to retire quickly. Anita didn't care about that at all.

But her former advisor focused his entire proposal on her retiring quickly.

And since Anita has never been retired before, how could she possibly know what she wanted to retire on—much less if $5,000,000 was the number she needed?

No wonder she was asking if it was enough.

I've worked in the financial planning industry for over thirty years, and here's something I've come to know about myself as well:

I have no idea how much I'll need when I'm retired either.

No One Knows How Much Cash They'll Need In Retirement

Listen.

It's not because I can't figure out the math.

After many years and so many clients, it's second nature for me. I can pretty much run the numbers in my head.

But, like Anita, I've never actually been retired before. I can't imagine I'll ever want to retire though. I love my clients, and enjoy helping them. Why would I want to retire from that?

I have however, seen a lot of what's worked (and not worked) for many other doctors and it's through that lens I asked Anita my next question.

"Anita, which would you rather do:

Save most of your income in order to retire as early as possible? Or save a little less and spend a little more as you work a few years longer?"

She smiled and said, "I love being a doctor. I think I'd always want to be working at least a little bit."

Her answer had nothing to do with how much she could save, or how much she wanted to spend in retirement. Anita didn't plan on working as hard as she could in order to leave a job she enjoyed doing. She wanted to retire younger BUT she also wanted to keep her hand in the game.

It wasn't about how big a pot she could grow, but how much and in which pot she needed to save to do the things she wanted to do when she wanted to do them.

My approach with Anita was different than she'd experienced with her banker.

Instead of showing how much she COULD save, we started to see how much she SHOULD save. Once we'd figured out her debt repayment plan, added in a healthy lifestyle budget, and ensured she was properly protected, we took what remained to be saved and cut that down by a third.

And so should you.

———•———

Strangely, Cutting 33% Of Your Planned Savings Makes More Sense.

Why did we do that? Let me ask you a question now.

Do you earn the same amount every month?

Or do your billings go up and down from previous months?

Or you have no billings at all when you take some time off or you're ill?

Since most of my clients' incomes vary each month, I don't like to plan for what they expect to average every month, but rather to save a portion of what they are most likely to earn in a month.

We go low vs high. Which is where the 33% savings reduction comes into play.

Once we had set up a strategic debt elimination plan for Anita, added on a healthy lifestyle budget, and got the right protection in place, what was left over—regardless of how she wanted to save—was to default her *ability* to save.

Knowing these numbers meant Anita was far more likely to hit her goals, but we took it a step further since I know her income changes month to month.

We determined the average amount she could save each month and set up an automated monthly savings plan.

This allows us to capture most of her expected income in a month, and as we meet throughout the year, the ups and downs of her income, as well as the ups and down of her spending, level out and we can see what she has remaining.

While Anita does occasionally have other ideas for her excess income, most times she chooses to add to her savings. To her, it feels like she's no longer working FOR her plan, but instead she's ACCELERATING her plan when she does these additional top-ups.

The answer to the question, "How much do you need to save?", is very personal to your planning.

But it's not about how big a pot you can grow.

We rolled up our sleeves and got to work with a more realistic plan that reflected what Anita wanted, not what she was being sold. Her plan worked towards a date when she could ideally work just a couple of days a week, and that made a huge impact on what she needed to save. Earning enough for her lifestyle was very appealing to Anita, and it meant we could target just over $3,000,000. And because she didn't need to save as much, it meant she'd be financially independent years earlier.

She didn't want to retire early of course. But Anita found it exciting that she could be more in control to work as much or as little as she wanted sooner.

So how much do YOU need to save?

The best way to answer is by instead asking, "How much do I want to spend, when do I want to start spending it, and how soon do I want to start saving towards that goal?"

Let's keep it simple by using a RSP and the rest you'll save within your Prof Corp, and your goal is to have $15,000 per month to spend (after-tax).

There are two factors you can't control:

1. Taxes. Your top marginal tax rate in Alberta in 2013? 39%. Just a few years later, that number now sits at 48%. Those ineligible dividends you pay yourself from your company when retired? To have $15,000 per month in 2013, you'd be paying yourself about $230,000.

Today, you'd need to pay yourself almost $260,000. Future income tax increases are effectively a retroactive tax on your savings, as they just became more expensive to spend.

2. Inflation. I remember a conversation I had with a client years ago when I was working at a bank, who told me inflation didn't exist. I remarked that I remembered when bus fares were $0.15, and how now they were over $2. "Oh, that's just because wages and gas prices went up." "Absolutely correct, and that's inflation." I replied.

Do you know how much more you'll have to pull out of your savings every twenty years, at just 3% inflation? Double. You need to save to consider inflation in retirement as well.

There are three factors you can control:

1. Work part-time in retirement. I often see this, but rarely out of necessity. Most of my clients LOVE being doctors! They're not working because they need to, they're working because they want to. (But we still want this to be your decision from proper planning, rather than a financial necessity from not having saved enough.)

2. Spend less in retirement. The first few years of retirement I find to be the most expensive for my clients, as they get to try all the experiences they've looked forward to doing. Eventually though, you'll settle into a comfortable rhythm and lifestyle, with the occasional trip or property purchase. Typically, around five years into retirement is when I expect my clients to know what they really want to spend on average.

A great solution can be to ladder your spending, where you spend more in your earlier retirement years when you have the health for things like travel, and step it down as you age.

3. Go more aggressively with your investments. I like this option the least. Which is more likely for you to be able to do: consistently get a higher return, or work for two-three more years?

Biggest tip? Start saving early.

A 35-YEAR-OLD WHO WANTS to consider having $15,000 per month from age 60 to age 95 would need to start saving $145,000 per year.

A 45-year-old with the same goals? Almost double … $270,000 per year.

Retirement planning isn't like trying to find the biggest mountain you can climb.

It's about finding the mountain you want to climb, and return down safely. And the earlier you start, the easier you'll find climbing your mountain to be.

"One of us is in serious trouble!"

Chapter Summary Lessons:

1. Start saving early—it'll be an easier mountain to climb if you do.

2. Your savings rate comes from knowing your debt, lifestyle and risk management spending first.

3. Automate your savings with monthly contributions, but start lower than you think and top-up along the way.

CHAPTER 15

Four Saving Vehicles & Strategies

WHAT DO YOU THINK IS THE most important investment strategy to retirement success?

And it ensures you never outlive your savings and are forced to live in your adult child's basement?

Years ago, I asked this question of one of my clients, Richard. His answer is one I hear often:

"I want to live off the income, and not touch my capital."

This sounds pretty intuitive, doesn't it? As long as you only spend what you earn, you're never in danger of running out of money. Unfortunately, this commonly held view doesn't work very well.

"Richard, let me ask you a question. Do things you buy tend to go up every year?" I asked.

"Do they ever!" was his reply.

"Absolutely. Every year the amount you'll need to spend from your savings will increase, just to keep doing the things you like to do. In only ten years, with just a 3% inflation rate you'll go from needing $120,000 per year to over $160,000—and we're planning for over thirty years of retirement.

Richard looked a little ill at this point. I smiled, but kept going.

"If we peel off all the interest income you earn to just live on and not touch your capital? The only way you'll avoid having to take out *more and more* is if your investments increase their payouts by the same amount.

Richard … did you plan on working this long and this hard, and never touch what you've saved?"

You could see Richard's internal struggle.

On one hand, he liked the idea of always having his portfolio there to keep him secure. But on the other hand, he'd never thought he'd work so hard, only live off the interest and then eventually pass along all the capital to someone else.

It's like eating only the icing, but never getting any cake.

Sounds like a raw deal to me.

———•———

Here's what I believe is the most important thing to do to ensure your retirement's success:

Don't take money out of your investments when the markets are down.

Wait … what?

If you invested $50,000 and the markets dropped 10%? You're left with $45,000.

If your remaining $45,000 then gained 10%, would you be back to $50,000? Nope—10% of $45,000 is $4,500, and now you're back to $49,500. After a 10% loss, you need a little over 11% just to break even and hopefully that doesn't take long to achieve or worse, you need to then take some of your money out.

That's why it so important to avoid a loss, as your portfolio just wouldn't recover.

Buy yourself cheap peace of mind and set some cash aside.

I get that you want to avoid a loss. Warren Buffett says the first rule of investing is to not lose money. But not taking money out of your investments when the markets are down for your retirement income needs, how do you do that?

There's a key word I used … investments. Investments can go up or down, but SAVINGS don't. I like to see my clients with at least six months of needed income sitting in secure, but accessible, savings within their Prof Corp *before* we start investing or retirement planning.

Here's something I've learned in working with doctors: there's always a number they need to see sitting safely in their company so they can sleep at night.

Can you relate? What's your number?

While you're working, I like to see six months of emergency savings. But when you're retired, I like to see your buffer increased to two or three years of needed income, to protect your savings from a market downturn.

Whether you're working or retired, I always want to see you with some money set aside in a simple high interest savings account, or cashable *Guaranteed Investment Certificate* (GIC).

Your money won't grow much in these types of savings, but that's not their purpose. We want to ensure you have funds you can access through any market or work interruption.

Worldwide pandemics. Zombies. Aliens. War. Strange American presidents.

So Where Do You Begin To Invest Your Money?

There are many different ways to save, and lots of ideas and strategies I share with you in the chapters coming up.

It's important to understand the difference between an investment, and an investment *vehicle*. If you buy a rental property, that's an investment. But if you bought it personally or in your company, that's the *vehicle* you have used to purchase your investment.

For now, let's stay high-level on the four main types of investment vehicles:

» Non-Registered

» Retirement Savings Plans

» Tax-Free Savings Accounts

» Individual Pension Plans.

Non-Registered.

This is the easiest type of vehicle with the fewest moving parts. You simply pay your taxes on your income, pick your investments (stocks, bonds, mutual funds, rental properties etc), and you'll pay tax along the way on gains you realize and eventually, on the part of the gains when you sell. It's straight-forward, but not optimal as you'll have to pay taxes each year on any interest, dividends, or realized capital gains (you sold something at a profit).

Retirement Savings Plans (RSPs).

I remember one of my first clients I met when I left the banks. Heather and Paul were a young couple with a toddler, and as we put their plan together, Heather said to me,

"We've put money aside in our RSPs for a few years now. They haven't grown very much though."

I looked at her statement and immediately saw several problems.

First, while they'd dutifully saved $100 per month into their RSPs, that's what they were *contributing*. Unfortunately, their savings were just sitting in cash and not *invested*. Their funds were receiving a whopping 0.25% annual interest—no wonder they didn't see their savings growing! Their advisor had sold them on the need for an RSP, but *then they had been forgotten after the sale*. It was like the funds sat in a kid's piggy bank or were stuffed under a mattress.

The second problem I saw was how their contributions hadn't kept pace with their increase in income from when they were in school. Heather now practiced as a family doctor and made about $300,000 a year. Her husband Paul worked as a journeyman electrician and while his income wasn't yet where it would eventually be, it was still higher than when they'd set up their RSPs. Yet their contributions hadn't kept pace with their income increases and they were only saving $2,400 per year.

The third problem wasn't as obvious, but is something I've seen many, many times and was one of the main reasons I left the banking world. They'd been advised to open and start making contributions to their RSPs *when they had almost no taxable income.*

They were missing out on the primary reason you use an RSP. It's a tax deduction.

Your RSP Benefits Your Life In Four Areas

This was a product sale through and through, and was not done with their interests at heart. Boy, was I upset!

When you contribute to an RSP, you remain fully invested, as your contributions are made with pre-tax dollars rather than with what remains after the tax man has picked your pocket. If you have $1,000 and decide to put it into your RSP, you'll have the full $1,000 to invest. Better yet, you can reduce your taxable income by the amount you contribute to your RSP and save some serious tax.

For example, if you have $200,000 of taxable income and you put $20,000 into an RSP, you're taxed as if you only earned $180,000, saving about $8,500 in taxes. Quite the incentive!

There's a catch though.

While your investments in your RSP will grow without being taxed, your growth isn't tax-free. The government rides along with you and eventually takes a bite out of both your contribution and any gains when you take your money out of your RSP. They're a tax *deferral* vehicle, and what you eventually take out is fully taxable.

1. You can save your contribution room until you're in a high tax year.

You don't lose your contribution room (the amount you can contribute), it just adds up over the years and when you're in a higher tax year, you can catch up on all your previously missed years. I love that.

How much you can contribute to your RSP each year is based on the lower of either the yearly maximum set by the government, or 18% of your earned income. For an incorporated doctor, this usually means the amount you paid yourself as a salary. Dividends are a 'redistribution of wealth' and not considered earned income, and therefore do not create contribution room.

If you paid yourself $100,000 in salary, you could contribute up to $18,000 to your RSP. But if you paid yourself $200,000 in salary, you'd bump up against the maximum allowable ($30,800 in 2023, or what your 18% would be if you earned a little over $170,000).

2. Tax Deferral.

I've already mentioned you benefit from the tax you'd have otherwise paid growing in your pocket rather than sitting with the government. You also avoid the death-of-a-thousand-cuts from tax bites on your growth along the way as your growth is tax-deferred. Tax deferral is a lovely thing.

3. Money you contribute to a RSP is generally protected from creditors.

While the instances of doctors being sued are thankfully few and far between, they DO happen. Having your money secure from such an event can be a comfort for you.

4. You draw the RSP when you're in a lower tax rate.

The biggest benefit is you can take your funds out when you're in a lower tax rate and keep the difference between the rate you put your funds in and the rate you pay when you take them out.

That's why I was so upset for Heather and Paul. Heather would never be in a lower tax rate than the one she was in when she contributed, and would likely *lose* money when she eventually took her money out at a higher rate than when she contributed.

Paul would **definitely** lose money as he contributed when he had no tax (and therefore received no tax refund), but he'd have to pay tax when he eventually withdrew his money for retirement income.

Ouch.

Don't get me wrong—RSPs are a terrific savings vehicle ... when the time and circumstances are right for you and not for a bank's sales targets.

Tax-Free Savings Accounts (TFSAs)

On the opposite side of the savings coin are TFSAs.

As the name implies, your investments are now growing completely tax-free. No tax while your investments grow, and no tax when you withdraw. Unlike RSPs, you only need to be the age of majority in your province to have room to contribute whether or not you have any earned income. In 2023, you could have up to $88,000 of contribution room if you were an adult when they were launched in 2009—even if you'd been a starving student living on loans and instant ramen noodles the whole time!

There's a couple of catches however.

First, unlike RSPs, your contributions are made with *after-tax* dollars. Depending upon your tax rate, this can leave you with as little as half of your income to be put toward your investments in a TFSA. This is why, when I see an incorporated doctor with a TFSA, I take a closer look.

If you have excess personal money because you didn't spend as much as you normally do and you decide you want to throw it into your TFSA? No problem at all, go for it.

BUT if you were advised to, on top of your personal income needed for your lifestyle and debt repayment, *withdraw for the purpose of contributing into your TFSA*, then your accountant and I need to have a little chat.

I really like TFSAs. They remove one of the biggest headaches and uncertainties in financial planning—what your future tax bill will be. But I like them when you have a tax-free or tax-preferred event in your company so most of your income is in your pocket, and not the government's.

Fortunately, or maybe unfortunately, that problem is *also limited by the second catch.* Your current yearly contribution in 2023 is only $6,500. If you're making $300,000 or more, you're only able to tax-shelter a very small amount of your income.

Still, if your choice is to save $0.89 of each dollar you earn within your incorporated company, or $0.52 of that same dollar in a TFSA, which would you choose?

A little further into our planning, Heather asked me something I constantly hear.

"Adrian, is it better to contribute to our RSP now that we're working, or is a TFSA better?"

"Heather, all things being equal, they're identical." I replied.

Wait … didn't I just say one is pre-tax on the way in, while the other is no tax on the way out?

My reason goes back to the math we learned in elementary school: the order of multiplication.

Let's assume you're in a 25% tax rate now, and you want to save $10,000 to be taken out ten years later. We'll assume the same investments for the same rate of return of 5%, and if you're in the same tax rate, here's how things look when you go to get your money.

RSP: Your $10,000 was fully invested and growing without tax. Ten years later, it's grown to $16,300. That leaves you a little over $12,200 once you've paid your 25% tax on the entire amount.

TFSA: You first pay $2,500 (25% tax rate on your $10,000) and invest your remaining $7,500. Ten years later at the same rate, that's grown to … wait for it … $12,200.

Identical.

The answer of which to use isn't based on one being better than the other, they're based on how you answer these questions:

1. Will your tax rate be lower or higher than it is today?

If you think lower, such as when your debt is gone or children have moved out, then an RSP is the way to go as you'll save the high rate and pay the lower one. If you think your taxes will be higher in the future, then it's probably better to pay a lower rate now so you can avoid paying the higher rate later.

2. Will you possibly need to access your money earlier than expected for some emergency or interruption in your income?

If so, then the TFSA is the likely winner. Not because of the tax you'd pay when you access your RSP—we just established the net result would be the same. It's because unlike RSPs, money you take out of your TFSA gets added to your future TFSA contribution room. RSP contribution room, once used, is gone. You cannot add back what you took out without more contribution room being used.

My recommendation for RSPs and TFSAs:

Step 1: Save your RSP contribution room until you're in a higher tax bracket.

Step 2: Only contribute to a TFSA if you have excess salary you've paid yourself, or if you have a tax-free or tax-preferred event to get money out of your company. If this is happening consistently though, consider cutting back your income to what you need rather than making contributions *after* paying your highest tax rate.

Step 3: Consider your future tax bill when you retire. If you're going to be at a high rate then as well, or if it would force you to be in a higher retirement rate than you otherwise could be? You might want to give them a pass and save within your company instead.

Individual Pension Plans (IPPs)

Think of IPPs like an RSP on steroids. They're essentially a defined benefit plan for one person ... you. Contributions are based on actuarial tables, and are larger than the amount you could otherwise contribute to your RSP (and are deductible to boot). And if your savings in your IPP don't grow by 7.5%, you're able to 'top-up' your contributions to that number.

They're generally creditor-protected as well.

Your Professional Corporation

Remember. Your Professional Corporation is your savings best friend.

The best way I can think to describe saving in your company is to think of it like you would an RSP. If your personal tax rate is higher than the small or general business rate, and at 11% and 23% respectively I can guarantee you they are, you may want to save within your Prof Corp and take your funds out later when you need your savings like in retirement and you're hopefully in a lower tax rate.

You won't likely have income needs to support your children who are grown up, nor are you likely to have your mortgage payments to make. That doesn't necessarily mean your income needs, and therefore your tax rate, will be lower though. Once you're retired, every day is a Saturday and you have a lot more time and opportunity to spend.

Pretty much anything you can think of investing in personally, you can invest in within your Prof Corp.

Stocks, bonds, mutual funds, rental properties, commercial real estate—all are available to consider for investments.

But as always, there are catches.

First, Prof Corps are easy targets for a tax-hungry government. Not even ten years ago, the tax rate on the dividends you'd take from your company to fund your retirement were around 27%. Today? A little over 42%. People who'd only saved within their company just got a huge increase to their cost to access their savings.

Second, the government doesn't like you using the rules to your benefit, like saving much more of your income in your company over letting them wet their beak first when you invest personally.

A few years ago, the government introduced a passive income test, where if you had more than $50,000 of passive income (basically income derived from ways other than your work like rental income, investments, etc.), you'd start to lose access to your small business rate of 11%. Once you're past $150,000 of passive income—all of your small business rate is gone and you pay the general rate.

Yes. That sucks.

I know many advisors use this as some kind of boogeyman to get you to invest in what they're selling. Listen. I'm not keen on you paying a lot of tax unnecessarily either, but there's something they're not telling you.

When you pay more tax now, you pay less tax later. (Assuming rates stay the same)

If you only pay your small business rate now, later on, your retirement dividends you pay yourself as income are called "ineligible" dividends. (That simply means they're ineligible for the lower rate other dividends receive.)

If, however, you paid the higher corporate tax now, your dividends are "eligible" for the lower dividend rates later.

Remember my lesson on whether RSPs or TFSAs were better? Well, as long as tax rates don't change, the same thing applies here. Less tax now, more later or more tax now and less later. Potato. Potatoe.

I◆I Agence des douanes et du revenue blah blah...

1050 The Give Us Your Cash Tax Form
New and Simplified

1. How much money did you make
last year? Fill in the blank:
$_____

2. Send it to us.
Better in our pockets than yours.

Chapter Summary Lessons:

1. Don't invest until you have your emergency savings number met, typically for six months of needed income.

2. Avoid taking money out when the markets are down, you'll need a higher rate of return to break even. Better yet, invest more when the markets have a sale!

3. Your choices today are to preserve your choices tomorrow—if you have it all in what's the 'best' option today, it may not be the best option when tax rates change in the future.

CHAPTER 16

Should You Borrow to Invest?

IN GENERAL, THERE ARE TWO TIMES when it's not a good idea to borrow to invest:

When you can't afford it, and when you can.

Okay, I grant there are times where the use of debt to buy an asset makes sense. Two scenarios leap to mind.

Unless you're walking around with a cool $500k or more to buy your first home, most of my clients use the bank's money through a mortgage they repay over time.

The other asset debt often purchased is your education. It's quite common for a new client of mine to have $250,000 or more of student loan debt for med school, which has purchased a very valuable asset—their ability to work as a doctor.

But there's a difference between borrowing for an asset that serves a purpose not already covered by your income, and borrowing to invest to grow, well … your investments. While you hope your home will appreciate, it's an asset you live in. Investments on the other hand, are only for the purpose of growing your nest egg.

So back to my earlier statement of when you can't and when you can.

If you can't afford the potential loss, you definitely shouldn't borrow to invest. If your plan will work without borrowing to invest, there's no point to taking on additional risk in achieving your goals.

Take the gambling out of your retirement plan. You work too hard for your money, and you've taken too much risk to get where you are now.

———————

Meet John. He Was In The Danger Zone.

A friend of mine, John, met with me for coffee one day after work. We've known each other for years on the dragon boat team I was coaching. I knew he was a doctor, but it wasn't until recently he found out I work with doctors. He had a bunch of questions about something his advisor had sold him, and we sat down to discuss his portfolio.

"My advisor told me I can do much better by making my contributions tax-deductible." John said.

"Oh—are you meaning making monthly contributions into your RSP?" I asked.

"No, we took out a $500,000 loan to invest in a regular investment account, and instead of making non-deductible contributions to it, I make loan repayments where the interest is tax-deductible. And because I'm in such a high tax rate, I'm getting like half off of my interest payments!"

Outwardly I cringed … inwardly I seethed at what his advisor had recommended.

I can guarantee you, if it hasn't happened already, that someone will come to you while you're working and tell you it's a great idea to borrow to invest. Don't do it.

On the surface, it sounds great.

You borrow to invest a lump-sum today that will *supposedly* grow faster than slowly investing over time, and the interest payments you make on your loan you can deduct from your income tax. In Alberta, that would reduce your interest costs between roughly one quarter and one half. Investing a lump sum to fully grow today should mean a bigger number at the end, when compared against a smaller amount invested over time. It's a no-brainer!

Or is it?

There's a lot more to this story than what John had been told.

Let's look at what happens if everything John said worked out as promised, so we can see what it might look like if (I'd say "when") it didn't.

Worse, there are things I saw in his portfolio that were going to make John pretty upset, which I'll get to in a moment.

How John Was Misled

We'll use a 5% rate of return, and all funds are in growth stocks so we avoid any tax leakage along the way. We'll also use the same 5% for his illustrated loan interest, so we can try to go apples to apples, and I'll even use the highest tax rate deduction.

If everything came up roses for John?

With a $500,000 loan at 5% over ten years, John would need to pay $5,300 every month. His total interest costs over the next ten years would be $136,400, and if John was in the highest marginal tax rate (as John's projection showed) at 48%, then he would be net out of pocket by $68,200.

His $500,000 on the other hand, would grow to about $814,500.

Taking off his total paid of $568,200 ($500,000 loan and $68,200 of net interest), John would look at a tidy gain of $246,200.

A good chunk of change ... what could go wrong?

Plenty, actually.

"John, I have a few questions for you about what I'm seeing here. First, what salary are you paying yourself from your company? This chart shows you at the 48% tax rate, but that's after about $305,000 of personal income (this was a few years ago … it's gone up since then!) You're making $300,000, so are you taking out more than all of your income from your company?"

John replied no, he was paying himself $15,000 per month ($180,000 per year), including what he needed to pay in taxes.

In 2017, that put him just over a 30% tax rate, not 48%. The 48% projection had been used to make the interest deductions look big.

"Here's another question, John. Markets go up, and they also go down. How are you going to feel if we have a sudden market drop like we had ten years ago and you see your investments are lower than the amount of your loan?" I asked.

A sick look came across his face. "I wouldn't feel very good about that. I'd probably want to sell I guess."

"You're really not going to like my next question then … do you know what the "DSC" stands for behind your investments?"

"Yeah, my advisor told me that was a way for me to invest without a charge, and as long as I hold the investments for ten years of the loan there won't be a charge to sell." John replied.

"It stands for *Deferred Sales Charge*, and it can be as high as 5.5% and usually takes seven years to tick down to zero. John, how would you feel if next year the market were to drop and you wanted to get out of this, but then saw there was a $25,000 penalty on top of your losses?" I asked.

"I would be very angry!" John was getting visibly upset.

"I'm sorry to tell you this, but did you know you could have had the same funds without a charge to buy or sell, even from the beginning?"

"No, I thought that's what I was buying." he said.

More cringing outwardly, and even greater seething inwardly for me. Fortunately, DSCs have now been banned in Canada, but you may still see some that were sold initially that way.

"Did he at least show you what just investing your same $5,300 per month over ten years would grow to?"

"Nope ... but I think you're going to show me, Adrian."

I whipped out my financial calculator. (Yes. I'm a financial nerd and carry one with me on my phone. You'd be surprised how many times I need to make these kinds of calculations every day!)

"If you invested $4,760 (the amount he'd net pay on his loan after deducting his interest) per month over ten years with an annual interest rate of the same 5%, in ten years you'd have $739,145.

"In other words, John, you're taking on this risk of a loan and investments that can go down as well as up, for a difference of about $74,500.

John's coffee had gone cold.

"John, I just have one last question for you. Which would you prefer: this borrowing strategy to make $74,500, or at your rate of income, would you just want to work for five or six months more to save it yourself?"

"I'd rather just work and invest as I have income. I could start and stop my savings instead of having to worry about making yet another loan payment." John replied.

How John Got Out Of The Woods

We created a strategy to take advantage of his ability to redeem some of his portfolio each year without a fee and then started to attack his loan.

His loan would be gone in just over five years that way.

Then we'd flip his payments to build a separate investment portfolio—while we waited for a good opportunity to sell the rest of his borrowed portfolio without a charge.

John couldn't believe how relieved he felt. The half-million-dollar investment loan had been a monkey on his back. He referred me two other doctors, and we got them on the right path as well.

Look, at your income level you have an ability to save and you don't need to take on more risk with your investments than you already have.

Borrowing to invest does make money. But for who? It makes money for the advisor selling it to you as they pocket an up-front commission on the investment, trailing revenue on larger assets under management for a larger number of years, and they often get a slice of your loan interest to boot!

I call that a sh*t show.

I don't like borrowing to invest. I hope after John's experience you won't either.

———•———

Chapter Summary Lessons:

1. Borrowing to invest often doesn't benefit you as much as it does your advisor.

2. Know the net benefit after using realistic numbers, and balance it against the angst you may feel if markets dropped.

3. Just don't borrow to invest!

CHAPTER 17

Planning for a Family

SINCE I WORK WITH SO MANY newly practicing doctors, I often get asked about how best to plan for a maternity leave.

I absolutely love being asked this question. I know they're asking me because it's a goal that should be included in their planning.

But for me, it feels like I'm being brought into their trusted inner circle and they value hearing how we can financially plan for such a major life event.

And I'm also a dad.

I'm honoured to help.

———

Remember Rebecca and Tom? My clients from the bank who wanted to look at starting a family? We were having our year-end meeting and Tom looked a little nervous, but Rebecca sipped her coffee and gave me a grin.

"Okay, Adrian. We're going for it! We want to have a family by next year."

Tom jumped in. "But we need to know how much to save ahead of time—I've heard that kids can cost a million dollars."

I was thrilled for them.

"That's awesome! And Tom, you can breathe—kids don't cost you a million dollars."

There are three phases we need to plan and save for. So, let's roll up our sleeves and figure it out."

Both Tom and Rebecca looked relieved.

Hey. I'm a dad of two kids. I get it.

Kids do cost money. But often not in the way you'd think.

Preparing For A Maternity Leave

Could I ever relate to Rebecca and Tom's questions:

» how do we save for time away from work?

» what will our increased costs be?

» how would this impact our work afterwards?

My wife and I had welcomed our first child a year earlier and we wondered about having a second child. My wife is a professional geologist; she had a high income that we would be without, and at the same time I was also planning to start my own financial planning company to focus on the needs of doctors.

We'd always heard that children were expensive. So, we were surprised when we found our baby wasn't the boss of our finances the first year. We really didn't have many additional costs once we'd bought the basics like a crib and diapers (Oh. So. Many. Diapers.) And we had a ton of friends who also shared a bunch of kid stuff, which was awesome.

Surprisingly, our biggest expenses were travelling to family while my wife was on maternity leave. We both have family in Vancouver, and we also headed to see my sister in Sweden. But there were no additional costs for having a baby with us. Unless you count the extra luggage for all those diapers ….

Rebecca and Tom: Planes, Daycare, and Missing Income

It was the decrease to their household income that would have the biggest impact. *But this should not be confused with children being expensive.*

For Rebecca and Tom, starting a family would mean a year without Rebecca's income, while Tom would need to watch his hours as much as he could in order to be able to give her some much-needed breaks. The drop in income would only be temporary, and with their ability to save it really wasn't the extra expense we needed to plan for.

So, what were the biggest expenses we planned for?

1. **Vacations.** Getting three, four or five plane tickets can really add up. Airbnb and VRBO have become a terrific way to have the space they need once they get there though! We added in a yearly travel budget into their planning.

2. **A new car.** It isn't necessary when their kids were young, but they'll need a bigger car once they're bigger and they've added in being a taxi-service for them and their friends. We looked at a new car for Rebecca, and planned for a newer car for Tom in five years.

3. **Education.** Like many of my clients, their children go to an amazing private school and that doesn't come cheap.

And that's before they pay for university! We started to take out additional income now to avoid having to take a big hit later all at once.

4. **Childcare.** Whether they hire a nanny or have a childcare service, this can be pricey. Tom and Rebecca liked the idea of a nanny, and would start to ask their friends for recommendations once they were expecting.

Once we had worked out what their budget should be, the next step was to start saving.

First figure out savings and taxes

Because Rebecca was still unincorporated and they wanted to start a family over the next year, we decided to hold off getting incorporated since they would need to withdraw savings anyway. (It was 2009 and the Tax Free Savings Account (TFSA) became available.) So we opened two $5,000 TFSAs and put the rest of their savings in shorter-term investments and GICs.

That's another important consideration—what they were saving in. Their goal was to have the money available to them when they needed it, not to somehow double it over the next year. Investing outside of secure investments would also mean they could lose money they needed.

Having tax-free money from their TFSAs, and minimally-taxed money from their other savings, meant Rebecca was in a very low tax rate and would avoid having her maternity benefits from *Employment Insurance* being taxed. Combined with a planned $10,000 per month from Tom's Prof Corp, and they were now set. They had a budget, savings, and government benefits.

This was a heart decision, not a head one.

Because Rebecca anticipated she'd earn about $300,000 or so, it meant paying more in tax to remain unincorporated until after she returned from her future maternity leave. But Rebecca and Tom felt like their lives were quickly becoming complicated,—they wanted an uncomplicated approach to their planned maternity leave.

It was just what the doctor ordered (so to speak).

What amount do you need to save to start a family?

That depends on you, but here are five questions to consider.

1. What is your needed monthly income after tax, and what should be added to it?

2. Do you have a working spouse or partner?

3. What bigger-ticket items will you need to buy like a car, or buying or renovating your home?

4. Will you have any Employment Insurance benefits you could receive?

5. How long do you want to plan for being away, and do you anticipate working full or part time when you return?

While these may sound like questions you don't know the answer to yet—rest easy. I've helped many of your colleagues, and I'm a parent.

And you'll need more diapers than you think.

"Room, board, books, and tuition – I draw the line at corkage fees."

Future Educational Costs

I mentioned a moment ago how children's education is a big expense. For my wife and me, it's easily been our biggest expense and will be for many years.

How do you view paying for your children's education?

While this may seem like a relatively simple question, I've seen many answers to this over the years. All of them are valid, and often I see spouses and partners with different heated viewpoints.

Do you want your children to attend a charter or private school? Maybe you feel post-secondary education is a must, and you want to pay for all their university costs. Or maybe you feel your children will value their education more if they work and pay for it themselves. Some of my clients have chosen to pay for a first degree, while others find a hybrid and pay for a portion.

This is a personal decision, one where you and your partner may or may not be on the same page. It's also a decision you may view differently in a few years as you experience being a parent.

I recommend my clients to plan as if they were paying for private school and university costs, so their savings are available to them if that's how things unfold. If it turns out later, they don't need as much as they saved, they simply add their excess to their other savings.

RESPS. To Use Or Not To Use?

If you do plan on paying for some or all of your children's post-secondary education, then we need to consider if you want to open and save within a **Registered Education Savings Plan (RESP).**

The savings in a RESP can be put toward a wide range of educational costs: tuition and books; room and board; even a car.

Even which post-secondary school they can attend has opened dramatically from when RESPs were first launched, and now includes colleges, universities, and trade schools.

Since the Federal Government matches 20% of the first $2,500 per year you contribute ($500)—known as the *Canada Education Savings Grant*, or CESG), the money can grow tax-sheltered. It eventually can be withdrawn and taxed in your children's hands.

You may feel this is a no brainer.

This is another of those head versus heart decisions though.

Sometimes, choosing a RESP puts you into the Twilight Zone.

———·———

Meet Shaun and Leah. A Busy Family With a Busier Future.

My clients, Shaun and Leah, have five young children. Yes, you read that right.

Paying for their post-secondary education is a major focus for Shaun and Leah. The problem is, Shaun's already almost at the highest tax rate at 47%, and to take out their needed $12,500 to maximize their grants (5 x $2,500 per child) he'd need to pay about $11,000 in taxes first.

From a head perspective, it doesn't make a lot of sense for Shaun and Leah to pay $2,200 of income tax to get a $500 grant—and that's per child.

From the heart perspective, it's a great savings habit to start their RESP. Shaun and Leah place a lot of value on paying for their children's education.

They could simply accept this $11,000 yearly tax bill (five children at $2,200 per year of tax), which would be offset later when their children went to university. Income received from a RESP is taxed in your child's hands, and only on the portion above what you contributed since you didn't get a deduction when you made your contribution.

Or they could opt to save $21,000 per year (what they'd have after corporate tax on their $23,500) in his Prof Corp—$6,000 more per year than would be saved even with the grants in a RESP—and then pay for post-secondary education as it comes up.

We got creative! Because we wanted it all.

We came up with a rather creative strategy to get their CESG funding. I call it the Hybrid Educational Plan. The monies that would have been spent on tax are now growing for them at the same time. Here's how we did it.

We got their bank to make their contributions for them. Shaun and Leah opened a line of credit with their bank, and used it to make their $12,500 RESP contribution in December. Their interest charges of about $50 for that month were less than the $2,500 of grants they received, and a LOT less than the $11,000 of taxes they would have paid otherwise. The $23,500 they now didn't have to take out they were able to invest in Shaun's Prof Corp instead.

We planned to repeat this over the next nine years, and at a 5% annual return at the end this is how things might look:

- » RESP Savings = $188,700
- » Prof Corp Savings = $264,000
- » (Less) Line of Credit Balance = $157,000

This would put them over $100,000 ahead of simply contributing to their RESP.

But wait … don't we have to still pay back the line of credit?

Absolutely.

But by then their mortgage payments will have finished, and we'll switch their mortgage payments to then repay their line of credit instead. Or we can collapse the RESP with little or no tax when paid to their children, clear out the line of credit and keep the difference—plus all their Prof Corp savings they wouldn't have otherwise had!

The Hybrid Educational Plan isn't a strategy for everyone. It does involve the strategic use of debt.

But I think doctors should be shown all their options.

As I get to know you and your family, I can help recommend suggestions based on what is the best match for your head versus heart decision.

And what have I done for my own kids?

Well, that's another one of those accountant-gives-me-the-stink-eye things:

My wife and I have funded our children's RESPs despite being incorporated. Fifteen years later, and there's $120,000 sitting in the education plan that didn't restrict our monthly budget.

And I'll need boxes of Kleenexes vs diapers when I watch them graduate.

NOW THAT OUR OLDEST is 15, I've stopped contributing to his RESP. Why? Because the maximum CESG grant per child is $7,200. At $500 per year, that's 14.5 years and I've been able to gather all of the grants available. Now, I'll just keep that amount in my company and continue to save there for his education, without paying income tax.

Chapter Summary Lessons:

1. You and your partner may have different views on paying for your children's education. Both views should be respected.

2. The strategic use of debt could work for you.

3. Start saving early. Little contributions can turn into big savings effortlessly.

CHAPTER 18

You Can Do It!

I WROTE THIS BOOK TO EMPOWER you to make informed financial decisions that are best for your views, values, and goals. You invested thousands in med school, ate a ton of cheap noodles, and spent years studying. Let's leverage the heck out of that!

You can create harmony in finding a balance with your partner, and free yourself from the fear of making wrong choices once you understand your financial options.

I hope I've achieved my goal for you to see through the experiences of other doctors, and how your path is truly your own.

Whether you choose to follow your head, your heart, or somewhere in-between, there's no wrong answer when you're able to make an informed decision for what feels right for you. Your planning can really be this simple, once you've had the noise cleared away for you to focus on what really matters to you.

But you need to put the plan into action.

If you follow my simple process, you'll find your financial life far more manageable.

Creating a debt management strategy so you can sleep at night, then knowing what you need to earn vs what you can earn allows you to determine your work & life balance. Armed with those two numbers, you avoid being over or underinsured. And what you earn beyond those three needs can safely and confidently be directed toward your emergency savings and then toward your longer-term investments.

Let your head and heart guide the way!

———•———

Need Help With It?

Plan it, Keep it, Pay it Down, Protect it, and Save it.

The five principles of wealth are really that simple.

Did you connect with this book? Is it dog-eared with a few coffee stains? And you'd like to learn more?

Please reach out and let's see if there's a fit for us to work together. I'd love to help you! If you'd like to set up a complimentary time to meet, you can:

Call or text me: (403) 837-9344

Email me: adrian@playcheques.com

Visit my website: playchequeswealthmanagement.ca

Or simply use this QR Code:

I look forward to learning about you!

—*Adrian*

Acknowledgements

To THE MANY DOCTORS WHO HAVE invited me into their lives to build a plan unique to them, thank you.

I'd like to acknowledge the incredible help I received in writing this book from one amazing book coach—Kim Duke. Kim not only kept me focused and on track, but did so with genuine humour and encouragement. This book would not have happened without her.

I would also like to acknowledge my friend and colleague, Shelley MacIntyre, whose comments and viewpoints are so very much appreciated.

———•———

About Adrian George

ADRIAN PROUDLY WEARS THE NAME OF "financial nerd"—a title bestowed upon him by his clients. He loves educating and helping doctors create meaningful and solid financial plans. A Certified Financial Planner with over thirty years in the financial industry, Adrian's seen a lot of what works well while also knowing when to say "don't step there." He created his company playchequeswealthmanagement.ca to encourage doctors to leverage and enjoy the fruits of their labours.

His focus on the unique challenges and opportunities of medical professionals allows Adrian to capture the best creative strategies that have helped others. He removes the noise, highlights what will make the most impact, and uses his financial nerd powers to keep them on track as their lives evolve.

Adrian is a highly sought after presenter and has spoken to thousands of advisors in Canada and the U.S. on how to truly listen, understand and engage with their clients, and how to always keep clients at the centre of their planning.

He loves to volunteer. From the Canadian country chair of the *Million Dollar Round Table* (the top advisors in a global organization of 85,000 members), to being a board member of the *Conference of Advanced Life Underwriters* (the highest/hardest association in Canada to be a member of), and being the coach for the *Children's Wish Dragonboat* team (now Make a Wish) which fundraised over $500,000 in ten years for children with life-threatening illnesses.

Adrian is based in Calgary, Alberta and when he isn't with clients, you'll find him exploring and enjoying life with his wife Stacia, and their boys Damian and Cameron. (And he's pretty crazy about his dog and cat too.)

Made in the USA
Monee, IL
09 June 2024

58969222R00144